Why On
This Night?

Why On This Night?

A Passover Haggadah for Family Celebration

BY
Rahel Musleah

ILLUSTRATED BY
Louise August

Kalaniot Books
Moosic, Pennsylvania

Table of Contents

How to Use this Haggadah

A NOTE TO PARENTS

What would a seder be without children reciting the Four Questions and chanting *Dayyenu*? As parents and grandparents we listen proudly when they chant the ancient words. Often, however, that's where their participation begins and ends.

This haggadah takes children beyond that limited role and gives them a central part in leading, participating, and questioning— empowering them to create a seder *they* can understand and enjoy. Through song, dance, drama, explanation, and action, this haggadah involves children in every step of the seder. It is not meant to distract children with puzzles and games while the adults go on with the "important stuff." Instead it makes children an integral part of the process.

Thousands of versions of the haggadah have been published throughout the centuries—scholarly texts, illuminated manuscripts, and vegetarian, women's, and egalitarian editions. You may already have a haggadah you love and wish to use at your seder. If so, think of this version as a companion: Let children peruse it silently, and invite them to read from it aloud at various junctures, perform the play, do the activities, or ask the questions to provoke discussion. Plan the seder with your children. Flip through this haggadah beforehand and decide together which parts they can lead. You may want to choose some parts for the first seder and, if you have a second seder, different parts for the second seder.

This haggadah can also serve as the main text at your seder. It weaves both spiritual and practical threads together to form the exciting and colorful fabric of a family seder. It contains many creative facets as well as basic elements of a traditional seder. To give the rituals depth and poetry, it provides explanations instead of simply listing directions like "Wash hands" or "Dip the green vegetable." And because the seder is designed to encourage conversation, each section of the haggadah features questions to spark discussion around your table.

Most seders have a leader. The leader can be anyone. While a parent or grandparent will often be the leader, let children feel they can be leaders, too. Directions throughout this haggadah will indicate the leader's parts. In all other segments, it is often most fun to go around the table and let each person have a turn to read the next section aloud.

This haggadah offers Hebrew text, English translation, and transliteration, making it accessible to those of all backgrounds. Nobody should feel left out! The gender-neutral translations remain true to the Hebrew text and try to convey its spirit at the same time. The most obvious example is the use of "Adonai," the original Hebrew word for God, instead of a term like "Lord." A few of the texts are abridged to make the seder "do-able" for families with children.

The excitement of the seder lies in its variation from one family to the next, from one tradition to the next. Use this haggadah as the foundation and inspiration for your own seder. It is an invitation to celebrating Passover with joy and meaning.

—Rahel Musleah

Key to Transliteration

(Based on the Jewish Publication Society Style Sheet)

Vowels:

a   as in farm
e   as in fed
o   as in hope
i   as in hit or street
u   as in flute
ei ay as in hay
ai as in eye

Consonants:

tz as in rabbits
h   (hay) as in hello
ḥ   (het) as in Bach
kh (khaf) as in Bach

Prefixes are separated by dashes. Adjacent vowels and consonants in two separate syllables are separated by an apostrophe.

Introduction: Celebrating Freedom

A kite soars high in a cloudless sky.
No one pulls it to the ground.
A child turns cartwheels in the grass.
No one restrains her joy.
That's how freedom feels.

Freedom gives us the power to choose how to live our lives,
which foods to eat,
which clothes to wear,
which schools to attend,
which friends to make,
which God to pray to.

Thousands of years ago, the Jewish people didn't know that joyous feeling we call freedom. They were slaves in Egypt crying out to be free.

Imagine a narrow prison cell, so tiny that our stretched-out arms touch the sides, and we have to sit huddled up, knees bent, in a tight ball. That's how slavery feels.

The seder is the story of the Israelites' journey from slavery to freedom. Everything we do on Passover reminds us of that awesome journey that began in the darkness of Egypt in the middle of the night and ended in a land the people had never seen, the land God had promised them, the land of Israel.

On Passover, we look forward to walking again on that road to freedom as if we ourselves were there.

Preparing for Passover

The seder is held on the first night of Passover, the fifteenth of the Hebrew month of Nisan. Many people also hold another seder on the second night. But preparing for Passover starts days, even weeks, before.

When the Israelites left Egypt, they escaped in a hurry. They didn't have time to bake real bread, only a flat bread called matzah. To remember that, we clean our homes of *ḥametz*: dough that doubles into yeasty breads, batter that rises into fluffy cakes, or anything else made with leaven—flour and water that mix together and ferment for more than eighteen minutes. So throw out that stale bagel! Waffles? Pretzels? Oatmeal-raisin cookies? We have to finish them before Passover.

As we sweep the crumbs from the corners of our rooms, we also clear our hearts of the crummy thoughts we have of others. We brush away the "outside" *ḥametz* and the *ḥametz* within us—all the puffed-up thoughts we have of ourselves: feeling that we're better than others or that we know more, feeling that nothing we do is wrong or that no matter how much we have, it's never enough.

We put away the dishes on which we eat peanut-butter-and-jelly sandwiches, and the pots and pans we use to cook spaghetti, and replace them with dishes used just on Passover. We fill our closets with special foods free of *ḥametz*.

Matzah, matzah everywhere!
Break it into bits—matzah crackers and matzah farfel.
Grind it up—matzah meal!
Turn it into other foods—matzah balls, matzah pudding,
even kosher-for-Passover pancake mix!
It's easy to taste and feel how different Passover is
from any other time of the year.

בְּדִיקַת חָמֵץ
Bedikat Ḥametz
Search for the Ḥametz

The night before Passover,
by the light of a candle in a grown-up's hand,
search for *hametz* throughout the house.
Sweep it onto a wooden spoon
with a feather—a kind of mini-broom.
We will burn the *hametz* in the morning.

Before the search, say:

בָּרוּךְ אַתָּה יהוה אֱלֹהֵינוּ מֶלֶךְ הָעוֹלָם,
אֲשֶׁר קִדְּשָׁנוּ בְּמִצְוֹתָיו וְצִוָּנוּ עַל בִּעוּר חָמֵץ.

Barukh atah Adonai eloheinu melekh ha-olam,
asher kid'shanu be-mitzvotav ve-tzivanu al bi'ur ḥametz.

Praised are You, Adonai our God, Ruler of the Universe,
Who has commanded us to remove all *hametz*.

Shh! The house is dark, wrapped in quiet as whispery soft as the feather we're holding. We've hidden ten pieces of bread throughout the house in places like these: under a napkin, in the toaster, on a shelf, inside an envelope, in a pot, under a bowl, between two plates, and on three chairs.

A match bursts into flame with a crackle and lights the candle we'll use to search for the *hametz*. It shines on our faces and on every nook and cranny as we search the kitchen, the dining room and den, gathering up the bread with the feather and spoon. We tiptoe up the stairs, giggling, to search the bedrooms and the rest of the house. Everything is clean, scoured free of crumbs. Tomorrow we'll burn the *hametz* we've collected, a miniature bonfire of bread. We're ready for Passover!

כָּל חֲמִירָא וַחֲמִיעָא דְּאִכָּא בִרְשׁוּתִי דְּלָא חֲמִיתֵהּ וּדְלָא בְעַרְתֵּהּ וּדְלָא יְדַעְנָא לֵיהּ לִבַּטֵּל וְלֶהֱוֵי הֶפְקֵר כְּעַפְרָא דְאַרְעָא.

Kol hamira va-ḥami'a d'ika vir'shuti, d'la ḥamitei u-d'la vi-artei, u-d'la yedana lei, li-batel ve-le-hevei hefker k'afra d'ar'a.

May all the *ḥametz* that I have not seen or removed
become like the dust of the earth.

◆ Try this!

Snap a mental photograph of the rooms in your house. Can you find five places *ḥametz* always hides? Erase that picture and snap one of yourself. What kinds of *ḥametz* hide inside you? It's easy to find the "outside *ḥametz*." Finding the "inside *ḥametz*" is much harder!

Set the Seder Table

Remembering the Israelites' journey from slavery to freedom is serious, important, and sometimes solemn. But it's not supposed to be boring. Picture the seder as a game. The haggadah is the instruction book and the seder table is the game board. Seder is a Hebrew word that means "order," and haggadah means "telling." The haggadah tells us that the game follows a special order.

Here is a list of pieces needed to play the game:

- a haggadah for each person
- candles and candlesticks
- bottles of wine and grape juice
- wine glasses for each person,
    for the four cups of wine or grape juice
- seder plate
- three matzot, covered with a matzah cover and placed to the
    right of the seder plate or behind it
- pillows for reclining
- salt water or lemon juice for dipping *karpas*
- pitcher of water, bowl, and towel for washing hands
- tablecloth, dishes, silverware, and glasses
- flowers or centerpiece
- cup for Elijah, filled with wine or ready to be filled
    at the end of the seder
- bag or cloth for the *afikoman*

Often, the directions in the haggadah will say, "Go to the seder plate," a big, round platter called a *k'arah*. It is filled with foods that help us remember the meanings of Passover. Before the seder begins, arrange the seder plate as shown on pages 16-17.

בֵּיצָה

Beitzah, **a roasted or hard-boiled egg**
(We don't eat the egg from the seder plate, but many
people eat hard-boiled eggs near the beginning of the seder.
It's a good way to fill growling stomachs!)
The egg symbolizes both the festival sacrifice and the hope for a fresh start in
life. Like chicks breaking out of fragile shells, wobbling slowly on uncertain
legs and then mastering a sturdy strut, so the Israelites learned to be free,
wobbling at first, then walking tall and strong.

כַּרְפַּס

Karpas, **a vegetable, usually one that's green**
(Celery leaves or parsley. Some people whose families are
from Eastern Europe use boiled potatoes, since green
vegetables were not available at Passover time.)
On the brown, wintry face of the earth, tufts of grass sprout
like green beards. Passover is also known as *Ḥag Ha-aviv,*
the festival of spring, because it replaces winter's bleak
mask with spring's cheery face.

מָרוֹר

Maror, **bitter herbs**
(Romaine lettuce or horseradish)
That pungent stuff called horseradish clears our noses in one
sniff. Those leaves of romaine lettuce have a crisp, strong flavor.
Both give us a small but unforgettable taste
of the bitterness of slavery.

The Seder Plate

זְרוֹעַ

***Zero'a*, a roasted bone**
(Some people use a raw or roasted beet.)
Long ago, instead of synagogues in every town,
one big Temple stood in the city of Jerusalem in Israel. It was
called the *Beit Ha-mikdash*. Jews from all over Israel came to the
Beit Ha-mikdash three times a year, on the holidays of Passover
(*Pesaḥ* in Hebrew), *Shavuot*, and *Sukkot*. Instead of praying
to God in words as we do today, they offered sacrifices
of animals. The *zero'a* reminds us of the lamb that was
sacrificed both on the night of the exodus from Egypt and
on Passover in the *Beit Ha-mikdash*. But *zero'a*, which
means "arm," also recalls the way God stretched out
an arm to free the Israelites from slavery.

חֲזֶרֶת

***Hazeret*, second bitter herb**
(Lettuce or grated horseradish)
Use this for the Hillel sandwich later in the seder.

חֲרֹסֶת

***Haroset*, a mixture of fruit and nuts**
Although *haroset* is sweet—made of fruits from apples to dates,
sometimes spiced with cinnamon and wine and
sprinkled with nuts—its brown
mixture is like the mortar the
Israelite slaves used when they made
bricks to build Egyptian cities.

Be creative! You can also add items to your seder plate to
symbolize issues important to your family. For example, many
people put an orange on their seder plate to acknowledge the
diversity and inclusiveness of the Jewish community.

Ḥaroset Recipes

Make the seder game even more fun by chopping nuts and apples for *ḥaroset* or creating a new recipe; by decorating pillowcases for the reclining pillows or turning clean white handkerchiefs into matzah covers; by designing placecards, a beautiful centerpiece, or miniature seder plates for each guest.

Here are three recipes for *ḥaroset* from different parts of the world. Ask an adult for help with parts of these recipes that may require sharp knives or cooking over the stove.

Ashkenazic Ḥaroset

Mix together:

2 large apples, chopped fine or grated
½ cup walnuts, chopped fine
½ teaspoon cinnamon
2 tablespoons sweet red wine

Add ½ cup raisins or any other dried fruit for a more creative recipe. If you do, add an extra tablespoon of wine and ½ teaspoon cinnamon.

Sephardic Ḥaroset

3 pounds pitted dates, soaked overnight in water
8 tablespoons sweet red wine
cinnamon to taste
chopped walnuts to taste

Put dates in a saucepan. Add water to cover dates. With help from an adult, simmer the dates on a low flame, stirring until dates are soft. Process in food processor or press through colander until smooth. Add wine, cinnamon, and nuts.

Ḥaroset "Yerushalmi"

1 cup pecans	1 cup dates	1 tablespoon cinnamon
1 cup almonds	1 cup white raisins	1 teaspoon ginger
1 cup walnuts	1 cup black raisins	2 teaspoons cardamom

With an adult's help, finely grind the nuts in a food processor and set aside. Next, put the pitted dates and raisins in the food processor and add a small amount of grape juice and a handful of the finely ground nuts so the mixture doesn't get stuck on the blade. Grind until there are no big pieces. Combine the nuts and fruit with your hands in a big bowl. Add the spices and mix, adding more liquid if needed. Pat into a rectangular container and refrigerate for at least an hour or up to several days in advance. Cut into bricks and stack.

Make Your Own Decorations

Place Cards

Fold unlined index cards in half. Write each guest's name on a card and decorate with pictures from the Passover story.

Seder Plates

Draw the Passover symbols on a paper plate. Paste muffin cups near each symbol. Decorate the rest of the plate any way you want. Fill each muffin cup with small portions of *zero'a*, *karpas*, *ḥaroset*, *ḥazeret*, *beitzah*, and *maror*.

Matzah Covers and Pillowcases

Decorate a white handkerchief or a clean white pillowcase
with crayon or fabric markers. If you use crayon, cover the finished
handkerchief or pillowcase with waxed paper, waxy side down. Ask an
adult to help you iron it carefully to set the illustration. You can also
embroider a design or sew on felt shapes.

Elijah's Cup

Set aside a large, clear plastic cup with a stem. Cut tissue paper of
different colors into squares. In a bowl, mix glue and water so the glue
becomes thinner. Paint the plastic cup with the watered-down glue. Stick
on the tissue paper squares. Paint over with glue to make it shiny.

הַדְלָקַת נֵרוֹת
Hadlakat Nerot
Light the Candles

The table is set and everything is in its place. Before the sun sets, light two candles. Some families light additional candles for each child. Say the blessing, adding the words in parentheses on Shabbat.

בָּרוּךְ אַתָּה יהוה אֱלֹהֵינוּ מֶלֶךְ הָעוֹלָם, אֲשֶׁר קִדְּשָׁנוּ בְּמִצְוֹתָיו וְצִוָּנוּ לְהַדְלִיק
נֵר שֶׁל (שַׁבָּת וְשֶׁל) יוֹם טוֹב:

Barukh atah Adonai eloheinu melekh ha-olam,
asher kid'shanu be-mitzvotav ve-tzivanu
le-hadlik ner shel [Shabbat ve-shel] yom tov.

Praised are You, Adonai, our God, Ruler of the universe,
Who has commanded us to light the (Shabbat and) holiday candles.

• Close your eyes and think of a wish for the holiday. Now open them. The flames shimmer yellow, orange, and blue with the warmth and beauty of Passover.

קַדֵּשׁ וּרְחַץ
Kadesh, Urḥatz
Order of the Seder

The seder is about to begin! But there are so many things to remember. What comes first? What goes next? What comes after that?

Sing or say this Hebrew rhyme that spells out the fifteen steps in the seder. Everyone:

Kadesh	קַדֵּשׁ
Urḥatz	וּרְחַץ
Karpas	כַּרְפַּס
Yaḥatz	יַחַץ
Maggid	מַגִּיד
Roḥtzah	רָחְצָה
Motzi/Matzah	מוֹצִיא מַצָּה
Maror	מָרוֹר
Korekh	כּוֹרֵךְ
Shulḥan Orekh	שֻׁלְחָן עוֹרֵךְ
Tzafun	צָפוּן
Barekh	בָּרֵךְ
Hallel	הַלֵּל
Nirtzah	נִרְצָה

Kadesh	Recite the *Kiddush* and drink the first cup of wine or grape juice.
Urḥatz	Wash hands without saying a blessing.
Karpas	Dip the green vegetable into salt water.
Yaḥatz	Break the middle matzah. Hide the larger half— the *afikoman*.
Maggid	Tell the story of Passover. Drink the second cup of wine.
Roḥtzah	Wash hands, and this time, say the blessing.
Motzi/Matzah	Recite the blessings over the matzah.

Maror	Dip the bitter herbs into the ḥaroset and say the blessing.
Korekh	Make a sandwich of bitter herbs and matzah.
Shulḥan Orekh	Eat the Passover meal.
Tzafun	Find and eat the *afikoman*.
Barekh	Recite the blessings after the meal, drink the third cup of wine, and welcome Elijah the Prophet.
Hallel	Sing songs of praise.
Nirtzah	Drink the fourth cup of wine. The seder is over.

See you next year!

Kadesh Urḥatz

Moderately

Oriental Folktune

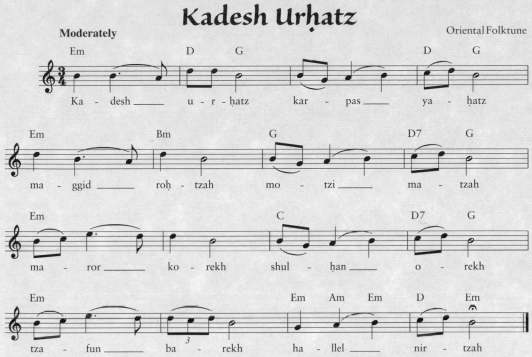

Kadesh ___ u – r – ḥatz kar – pas ___ ya – ḥatz

ma – ggid ___ roḥ – tzah mo – tzi ___ ma – tzah

ma – ror ___ ko – rekh shul – ḥan o – rekh

tza – fun ___ ba – rekh ha – llel ___ nir – tzah

Kadesh	Maror
Urḥatz	Korekh
Karpas	Shulḥan Orekh
Yaḥatz	Tzafun
Maggid	Barekh
Roḥtzah	Hallel
Motzi/Matzah	Nirtzah

קַדֵּשׁ
Kadesh
The First Cup

On a calendar, special days are often marked in red, setting them apart from other days of the week. An ordinary Monday becomes Presidents' Day. An ordinary Thursday becomes Thanksgiving.

Passover, too, is marked in red on the calendar. Another way to label it "special" is by making a blessing called *Kiddush*. The blessing says, "This day is different. This day is holy, set apart from ordinary days." We make that blessing over a goblet of wine or grape juice because wine is a sign of sweetness, freedom, and happiness.

Every Sabbath and Jewish holiday begins with *Kiddush*, recited over one cup of wine. But on Passover, we drink four cups to match four phrases in the Bible that describe the ways God would free the Jewish people. God said:
"*Ve-hotzeiti*: I will bring you out of Egypt."
"*Ve-hitzalti*: I will free you from slavery."
"*Ve-ga'alti*: I will save you with My outstretched arm."
"*Ve-lakaḥti*: I will take you to be My people."

To show that we are slaves no longer, someone else at the table fills our cup with wine or grape juice so that it almost overflows, brimming with joy and thanks. When we finish saying the blessings we drink the wine, relaxing against soft pillows and leaning to the left. (Long ago, people thought that was the best way to digest food!) That's how we embrace the downy comfort of freedom.

The leader lifts the cup of wine and says:
(On Shabbat, add the words in parentheses:)

(וַיְהִי עֶרֶב וַיְהִי בֹקֶר יוֹם הַשִּׁשִּׁי. וַיְכֻלּוּ הַשָּׁמַיִם וְהָאָרֶץ וְכָל צְבָאָם: וַיְכַל
אֱלֹהִים בַּיּוֹם הַשְּׁבִיעִי מְלַאכְתּוֹ אֲשֶׁר עָשָׂה, וַיִּשְׁבֹּת בַּיּוֹם הַשְּׁבִיעִי מִכָּל
מְלַאכְתּוֹ אֲשֶׁר עָשָׂה: וַיְבָרֶךְ אֱלֹהִים אֶת יוֹם הַשְּׁבִיעִי וַיְקַדֵּשׁ אֹתוֹ, כִּי בוֹ שָׁבַת
מִכָּל מְלַאכְתּוֹ אֲשֶׁר בָּרָא אֱלֹהִים לַעֲשׂוֹת.)

(Va-yehi erev va-yehi voker yom ha-shishi.
Va-yekhulu ha-shamayim ve-ha'aretz ve-khol tzeva'am.
Va-yekhal Elohim ba-yom ha-sh'vi'i melakhto asher asah,
Va-yishbot ba-yom ha-sh'vi'i mi-kol melakhto asher asah.
Va-y'varekh Elohim et yom ha-sh'vi'i va-y'kadesh oto,
Ki vo shavat mi-kol melakhto asher bara Elohim la-asot.)

(On the sixth day, God completed the heavens and the earth.
On the seventh day, God finished creating the universe and rested.
God blessed the seventh day and made it holy.)

בָּרוּךְ אַתָּה יהוה אֱלֹהֵינוּ מֶלֶךְ הָעוֹלָם, בּוֹרֵא פְּרִי הַגָּפֶן.
בָּרוּךְ אַתָּה יהוה אֱלֹהֵינוּ מֶלֶךְ הָעוֹלָם, אֲשֶׁר בָּחַר בָּנוּ מִכָּל עָם וְרוֹמְמָנוּ מִכָּל
לָשׁוֹן וְקִדְּשָׁנוּ בְּמִצְוֹתָיו, וַתִּתֶּן לָנוּ יהוה אֱלֹהֵינוּ בְּאַהֲבָה (שַׁבָּתוֹת לִמְנוּחָה וּ)
מוֹעֲדִים לְשִׂמְחָה, חַגִּים וּזְמַנִּים לְשָׂשׂוֹן, אֶת יוֹם (הַשַּׁבָּת הַזֶּה וְאֶת יוֹם)
חַג הַמַּצּוֹת הַזֶּה, זְמַן חֵרוּתֵנוּ, (בְּאַהֲבָה) מִקְרָא קֹדֶשׁ, זֵכֶר לִיצִיאַת מִצְרָיִם.
כִּי בָנוּ בָחַרְתָּ וְאוֹתָנוּ קִדַּשְׁתָּ מִכָּל הָעַמִּים, (וְשַׁבָּת) וּמוֹעֲדֵי קָדְשֶׁךָ
(בְּאַהֲבָה וּבְרָצוֹן) בְּשִׂמְחָה וּבְשָׂשׂוֹן הִנְחַלְתָּנוּ. בָּרוּךְ אַתָּה יהוה מְקַדֵּשׁ
(הַשַּׁבָּת וְ) יִשְׂרָאֵל וְהַזְּמַנִּים.

Barukh atah Adonai eloheinu melekh ha-olam, borei p'ri ha-gafen.
Barukh atah Adonai eloheinu melekh ha-olam, asher baḥar banu mi-kol
am ve-rom'manu mi-kol lashon ve-kid'shanu be-mitzvotav.
Va-titen lanu Adonai eloheinu be-ahavah (Shabbatot li-m'nuḥah u-)
mo'adim le-simḥah, ḥagim u-z'manim le-sasson, et yom (ha-Shabbat
ha-zeh ve-et yom) Ḥag Ha-Matzot ha-zeh, z'man ḥeruteinu, (be-ahavah)
mikra kodesh, zekher litziyat Mitzrayim. Ki vanu vaḥarta ve-otanu
kidashta mi-kol ha-amim, (ve-Shabbat) u-mo'adei kodsh'kha (be-ahavah
u-v'ratzon) be-simḥah u-v'sasson hinḥaltanu. Barukh atah Adonai,
mekadesh (ha-Shabbat ve-) Yisrael ve-ha-z'manim.

Praised are You, Adonai our God, Ruler of the universe,
Who creates the fruit of the vine.
Praised are You, Adonai our God, Ruler of the universe,
Who has lifted us up through *mitzvot*
and, with love, has given us (Shabbat for rest and) festivals for joy.
God has given us (Shabbat and) this Holiday of Matzot,
a celebration of freedom when we remember how we left Egypt.
Praised are You, Adonai our God, Who has set apart
(Shabbat and) the people Israel and the festivals.

(If Passover begins on Saturday night, add:

בָּרוּךְ אַתָּה יהוה אֱלֹהֵינוּ מֶלֶךְ הָעוֹלָם, בּוֹרֵא מְאוֹרֵי הָאֵשׁ.
בָּרוּךְ אַתָּה יהוה הַמַּבְדִּיל בֵּין קֹדֶשׁ לְקֹדֶשׁ.

Barukh atah Adonai eloheinu melekh ha-olam, borei me'orei ha-esh.
Barukh atah Adonai eloheinu melekh ha-olam, ha-mavdil bein kodesh
le-kodesh.

Praised are You, Adonai our God, Ruler of the universe,
Who creates the lights of fire.
Praised are You, Adonai our God,
Who separates the holiness of Shabbat from the holiness of festivals.)

The leader continues:

בָּרוּךְ אַתָּה יהוה אֱלֹהֵינוּ מֶלֶךְ הָעוֹלָם, שֶׁהֶחֱיָנוּ וְקִיְּמָנוּ וְהִגִּיעָנוּ לַזְּמַן הַזֶּה.

Barukh atah Adonai eloheinu melekh ha-olam,
she-heḥeyanu ve-ki'y'manu ve-higiyanu la-z'man ha-zeh.

Praised are You, Adonai our God, Ruler of the universe,
Who has given us life and kept us well
so we could celebrate this special time.

Everyone drinks the wine or grape juice, leaning to the left.

וּרְחַץ
Urḥatz
Wash the Hands

Wash your hands without reciting a blessing. Pass around a pitcher of water, a bowl, and a towel. Hold the pitcher in one hand and pour water over the other hand. Then reverse hands and repeat.

Hands that are spackled with paint, sticky with jelly, or muddy from digging in the garden need to be washed. But at the seder, dressed in crisp holiday clothes, our hands are not stained or soiled. So why wash them?

Think about the cool tickle of water over your fingers. As it cleans the body, it also wakes up the mind, helping us to appreciate that no food is ordinary. A carrot stick, a leaf of lettuce, a stalk of celery—all grew and reached our table with the blessings of God and the hard work of human beings.

Usually, when we wash our hands before eating, we say a blessing. We will do that later in the seder, but now we wash without a blessing. That's one of the things that makes this night different from all other nights!

כַּרְפַּס
Karpas
Eat the Green Vegetable

The seder's just started but everybody's already hungry. *Karpas* promises an appetizer. Dip the green vegetable, a sign of spring and hope, into salt water, vinegar, or lemon juice, to recall the tears of the Israelite slaves. (You may choose to follow the ancient custom of snacking on other vegetables at this time to help you through the seder. But save your appetite for the matzah!)

Before eating, say:

בָּרוּךְ אַתָּה יהוה אֱלֹהֵינוּ מֶלֶךְ הָעוֹלָם, בּוֹרֵא פְּרִי הָאֲדָמָה.

Barukh atah Adonai eloheinu melekh ha-olam, borei p'ri ha-adamah.

Praised are You, Adonai our God, Ruler of the universe, Who creates everything that grows from the earth.

The vegetables we use for *karpas*—parsley, celery, or potato—grow with their roots deep in the earth. They remind us of the earth. As we dip the *karpas* into the salt water—a small taste of the vast salty sea—earth and ocean come together. It's as if the *karpas* combination contains the whole universe. We can picture building a healthy world where water and soil are clean, pure, and free of pollution.

When parsley or celery pop out like green crowns on the earth, they remind us of spring, of all that is new and young and hopeful. But the salt water—the ocean—recalls all that is old, its waves rumbling back to the beginning of time. When we dip the *karpas* into the salt water, young and old, future and past, all come together at the seder. It's as if the *karpas* combination contains the whole universe, showing that both young and old are important in creating a whole, happy world.

Let's go back in time,
as if you and I had lived long, long ago. . . .

I remember when we left Egypt,
I held on to my grandfather's hand.
I helped him carry his bundle of food and clothes,
even though I could see the muscles in his arms
were still tight and strong.
When the bundles got heavy, he gave me hope.
He said we were traveling to a better world,
and to get there we had to cross land and sea.
Then he made me laugh!
He described the place we were going to
as a land flowing with milk and honey.
Can you imagine?

• Ask each guest at the seder to describe one way they could help make a better world.

יַחַץ
Yaḥatz
Break the Middle Matzah

The leader breaks the middle matzah—to share what we have with those who have less—and wraps the larger piece in a napkin. That's the *afikoman*. We'll eat it at the end of the seder. Then the leader puts the smaller piece back between the other two matzot.

Everyone sings together:

הָא לַחְמָא עַנְיָא
דִּי אֲכָלוּ אַבְהָתָנָא בְּאַרְעָא דְמִצְרָיִם.
כָּל דִּכְפִין יֵיתֵי וְיֵיכָל,
כָּל דִּצְרִיךְ יֵיתֵי וְיִפְסַח,
הָשַׁתָּא הָכָא, לְשָׁנָה הַבָּאָה בְּאַרְעָא דְיִשְׂרָאֵל,
הָשַׁתָּא עַבְדֵי, לְשָׁנָה הַבָּאָה בְּנֵי חוֹרִין.

Ha laḥma anya
Di akhalu avhatana be-ar'a de-Mitzrayim.
Kol dikhfin yete ve-yekhol.
Kol ditzrikh yete ve-yifsaḥ.
Hashata hakha, le-shanah ha-ba'ah be-ar'a de-Yisrael
hashata avdei, le-shana ha-ba'ah b'nei ḥorin.

This is the poor people's bread that our ancestors ate in Egypt. All who are hungry, come and eat. All who are in need, come celebrate Passover with us.

This paragraph is written in Aramaic. Long, long ago it was the language everyone spoke and understood. The seder is for all of us: rich and poor, young and old. No one is left out. We may not be slaves anymore, but we haven't forgotten what it's like to be hungry.

Let's go back in time again. . . .

I remember when all we had to eat for days were dry crackers.
You told me the crackers were called matzah.
*I liked the sound of the name . . . **Mmm** . . . atzah . . .*
*I savored every bite of its plain taste . . . **Mmm** . . .*
*Crunching noisily as I chewed . . . **Mmm** . . . atzah . . .*
I broke off a piece for you.
You broke it in two again, ate your half,
and hid the other half in your pocket.
"In case we meet somebody even hungrier than we are," you said.

Before Passover we collect money called *ma'ot ḥittin*
for all who are homeless and hungry,
so everyone will have enough to celebrate the holiday.
We invite people who are lonely to our seder table.

We think about people who are lonely and hungry on Passover, but we can help them during ordinary days also. A story about Rabbi Tanḥum, who lived long ago, tells us that every time he went grocery shopping, he'd buy two of everything: one for himself and one for poor people. Another story about Rabbi Huna tells us that every time he sat down to a meal, he'd open his door first and call out, "Let all who are in need come inside and eat."

Today, in Jerusalem and throughout the world—maybe even in your own neighborhood—people cook meals to feed people who are old and poor and lonely. Across the United States, men, women, and children collect food, shoes, clothing, and other supplies that might otherwise have been thrown away, and distribute them to poor and hungry people. Think of what we can do after the seder to help people who are poor or hungry.

The *afikoman* reminds us to save food for others, but breaking the middle matzah also provides a break in the seder. Now's a good time for a game. When nobody's looking, take the *afikoman* and hide it. All the grown-ups will have to look for it later.

Maybe your parents or grandparents will hide it instead, and you'll have to search for it. Whoever finds it might win a prize! Looking for the *afikoman* is like playing hide-and-seek, hunting for treasure, or acting the part of a detective. It's fun discovering something lost or something we didn't know before.

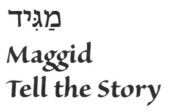

מַגִּיד
Maggid
Tell the Story

Imagine getting straight A's on a report card or scoring the winning goal in a basketball tournament. You'd feel like telling the whole world how hard you worked, how you didn't know what would happen until the last moment, how you felt like flying above the rooftops and shouting, "I did it!

Imagine a different time and place, full of bitterness and hope.
Imagine leaving Egypt. What a powerful story that would make!
How hard we worked under the taskmaster's whip!
We didn't know until the last moment whether we'd actually leave.
Now, in the warm sand of freedom, even our toes feel tingly, unbound.
We feel like flying above the rooftops and shouting, "We're free!"

That's the story we tell in the haggadah. Like our own family stories of how we were born, where we lived and when we moved, what we did as babies and toddlers and kindergartners, we've told the Passover story over and over because it's the story of our larger family—the Jewish people.

We've told it from parent to child, from grandparent to grandchild, for thousands of years after it happened, because it changed our lives. It molded us into a free nation, *Am Yisrael*, the Jewish people. Could there be a more powerful story?

• Share a family story you or your parents like to tell. It could be something funny you did when you were younger or something you did that makes you proud.

מַה נִּשְׁתַּנָּה
Mah Nishtanah
The Four Questions

There are many ways to tell a story. You can start with "Once upon a time" and end with "And they lived happily ever after." Or you can start with a question to get everyone's attention: "Did you ever hear the story of . . . ?"; "Do you know why . . . ?"

Sometimes a story isn't told in a straight line from A to Z. It meanders and curves and wanders and dips, like a flowing river. Sometimes it's interrupted by questions and comments and flows around them like water flows around stones in a river. That's the way the haggadah tells the story of Passover. The story begins with four simple questions.

Cover the matzot and fill the second cup.
The youngest child may recite the Four Questions,
or everyone may sing together:

מַה נִּשְׁתַּנָּה הַלַּיְלָה הַזֶּה מִכָּל הַלֵּילוֹת?

שֶׁבְּכָל הַלֵּילוֹת אָנוּ אוֹכְלִין חָמֵץ וּמַצָּה, הַלַּיְלָה הַזֶּה כֻּלּוֹ מַצָּה.

שֶׁבְּכָל הַלֵּילוֹת אָנוּ אוֹכְלִין שְׁאָר יְרָקוֹת, הַלַּיְלָה הַזֶּה מָרוֹר.

שֶׁבְּכָל הַלֵּילוֹת אֵין אָנוּ מַטְבִּילִין אֲפִילוּ פַּעַם אֶחָת, הַלַּיְלָה הַזֶּה שְׁתֵּי פְעָמִים.

שֶׁבְּכָל הַלֵּילוֹת אָנוּ אוֹכְלִין בֵּין יוֹשְׁבִין וּבֵין מְסֻבִּין, הַלַּיְלָה הַזֶּה כֻּלָּנוּ מְסֻבִּין.

Mah nishtanah ha-lailah ha-zeh mi-kol ha-leilot? She-be-khol ha-leilot anu okhlin ḥametz u-matzah, ha-lailah ha-zeh kulo matzah.

She-be-khol ha-leilot anu okhlin she'ar yerakot, ha-lailah ha-zeh maror.

She-be-khol ha-leilot ein anu matbilin afilu pa'am eḥat, ha-lailah ha-zeh sh'tei fe'amim.

She-be-khol ha-leilot anu okhlin bein yoshvin u-vein mesubin, ha-lailah ha-zeh kulanu mesubin.

Why is this night different from all other nights?
On all other nights we eat *ḥametz* or matzah.
Why, tonight, do we eat only matzah?

On all other nights we eat all kinds of vegetables.
Why, tonight, do we eat *maror*?

On all other nights we don't dip our vegetables—not even once!
Why, tonight, do we dip them twice?
(Once *karpas* in salt water and once *maror* in *ḥaroset*.)

On all other nights we eat sitting up straight or leaning
any way we want. Why, tonight, do we all lean?

Repeat in similar fashion for additional verses.

1. *Mah nishtanah ha-lailah ha-zeh mi-kol ha-leilot, mi-kol ha-leilot?*
   She-be-khol ha-leilot anu okhlin ḥametz u-matzah, ḥametz u-matzah,
   Ha-lailah ha-zeh, ha-lailah ha-zeh, kulo matzah.

How different this night is from other nights!
On many other nights our parents may get tired of our questions:
When are we going to get there?
Do I have to eat that?
Do I have to do that?
Why?
Tonight they want us to ask as many questions as possible.
Even if we were at the seder all alone,
we're still supposed to ask questions.

We do so many unusual things at the seder that questions fill our minds as fast as kernels of corn pop in the microwave. Why do we sometimes pretend we are slaves, eating only matzah and *maror*? Why do we sometimes act like kings and queens, dipping our food twice and leaning against pillows? How can we be both slaves and royalty?

On the night we left Egypt, we were poor slaves one minute and free people who felt like kings and queens the next. Slaves aren't allowed to ask questions. Free people can ask as many questions as they like.

• We don't have to stop at these four questions. Go around the table and have each person ask a new question. Here are some to get you started:

> *Why do we sometimes feel like slaves even though we are free?
> *What kinds of things happen in the world that are bitter like
>   *maror*? What can we do to sweeten them?
> *Would our lives be better if they were plain and simple, like
>   matzah, instead of full of *ḥametz*?
> *How can we dip into ourselves and give to other people to
>   make their lives better?

עֲבָדִים הָיִינוּ
Avadim Hayinu
Once We Were Slaves

Here are the answers to the Four Questions.

עֲבָדִים הָיִינוּ לְפַרְעֹה בְּמִצְרָיִם. וַיּוֹצִיאֵנוּ יהוה אֱלֹהֵינוּ מִשָּׁם בְּיָד חֲזָקָה וּבִזְרֹעַ
נְטוּיָה. וְאִלּוּ לֹא הוֹצִיא הַקָּדוֹשׁ בָּרוּךְ הוּא אֶת אֲבוֹתֵינוּ מִמִּצְרַיִם, הֲרֵי אָנוּ
וּבָנֵינוּ וּבְנֵי בָנֵינוּ מְשֻׁעְבָּדִים הָיִינוּ לְפַרְעֹה בְּמִצְרָיִם. וַאֲפִלּוּ כֻּלָּנוּ חֲכָמִים, כֻּלָּנוּ
נְבוֹנִים, כֻּלָּנוּ זְקֵנִים, כֻּלָּנוּ יוֹדְעִים אֶת הַתּוֹרָה, מִצְוָה עָלֵינוּ לְסַפֵּר בִּיצִיאַת
מִצְרָיִם. וְכָל הַמַּרְבֶּה לְסַפֵּר בִּיצִיאַת מִצְרַיִם הֲרֵי זֶה מְשֻׁבָּח.

*Avadim hayinu le-Pharoh be-Mitzrayim. Va-yotsi'einu Adonai Elohenu
mi-sham be-yad ḥazakah u-vi-z'roa netuyah. Ve-ilu lo hotzi Ha-Kadosh
Barukh Hu et avoteinu mi-Mitzrayim, harei anu u-vaneinu u-v'nei
vaneinu meshubadim hayinu l'Pharoh be-Mitzrayim. Va-afilu kulanu
ḥakhamim, kulanu nevonim, kulanu z'kenim, kulanu yod'im et
ha-Torah, mitzvah aleinu le-saper bi'tziyat Mitzrayim. Ve-khol
ha-marbeh le-saper bi'tziyat Mitzrayim harei zeh meshubaḥ.*

Why do we perform the Passover rituals? Because once we were slaves
to Pharaoh in Egypt. God brought us out of Egypt with a strong hand
and an outstretched arm.

Why did God need a strong hand *and* an outstretched arm? Wasn't a
strong hand enough, the strong hand of a fighter who could battle the
Egyptians? No. God needed to reach out to us at the same time, like a
lifeguard rescuing a swimmer, or a parent embracing a child. God had to
be both strong and gentle.

Do you remember when God rescued us?
We were afraid to leave Egypt. After all, it was our home,
even though it was an unhappy, miserable home.
It was midnight, and I remember you shivered in the blackness outside.
Then we heard God call, "Don't be afraid."
To me it felt like a powerful hand reached out through the darkness,
took hold of our hands, and guided us to safety.

Avadim Hayinu

Allegro moderato

A - va - dim ha - yi - nu ha - yi - nu a - tah b'nei ḥo - rin __ b' -

nei ḥo - rin a - va - dim __ ha - yi - nu a - tah a - tah b' - nei ḥo - rin __

a - va - dim __ ha - yi - nu a - tah a - tah b' - nei ḥo - rin b' - nei ḥo - rin

• To the tune of the song *Avadim Hayinu*, make up a dance of slavery and freedom, of strong hands and outstretched arms. Try this as an example:

Make a circle. Bend down low and walk around once (*avadim hayinu*, once we were slaves). Walk around the circle again. This time, throw your hands up joyfully (*atah b'nei ḥorin*, now we are free). Now make a fist as you walk around (*avadim hayinu*). Now let your fingers go, reach out for the person next to you, and link hands (*atah b'nei ḥorin*).

בָּרוּךְ הַמָּקוֹם
Barukh Ha-Makom
Praise for God

We pause in the story to praise God.
Sing or say together:

בָּרוּךְ הַמָּקוֹם. בָּרוּךְ הוּא.
בָּרוּךְ שֶׁנָּתַן תּוֹרָה לְעַמּוֹ יִשְׂרָאֵל. בָּרוּךְ הוּא.

Barukh Ha-Makom. Barukh hu.
Barukh she-natan Torah le-amo Yisrael. Barukh hu.

Let's praise God, Who is everywhere.
Let's praise God, Who gave us the Torah.

No superhero swooped down on Egypt to free the Jewish people.
God is the "hero" of the haggadah. Moses, who led us out of
Egypt, is not even mentioned in most haggadot.

The haggadah calls God *Ha-Makom*, "the place." God is a vast "place"
that includes the whole universe: From our kitchen to the Big Dipper,
from our school to the red spot on Jupiter, and everything in between
and beyond.

God means different things to different people at different times.
Sometimes we need God to help us be strong, like a rock. Sometimes
we need God to guide and comfort us, like a shepherd. So Judaism has
many names for God: *Adonai*, my Lord; Shepherd of Israel, Most High,
Rock of Israel, Maker of Peace, Guardian of Israel, Healer, Creator, The
Name. Though God is not a person, nor a wise old man or woman in
the sky, the names of God show different "faces" of God.

Some people believe that God knows everything they do. Some believe that God is not involved in their lives. The Torah and the haggadah tell us that God planned and directed everything that happened to the Jewish people in Egypt.

• Choose a name for God or make one up that describes how you feel about God.

אַרְבָּעָה בָּנִים
Arba'ah Banim
The Four Children

When we tell the story of Passover,
we try to see it through the eyes of four different kinds of people:
One is wise, one is wicked, one is simple,
and one does not know how to ask the right questions.

כְּנֶגֶד אַרְבָּעָה בָּנִים דִּבְּרָה תוֹרָה.
אֶחָד חָכָם,
וְאֶחָד רָשָׁע,
וְאֶחָד תָּם,
וְאֶחָד שֶׁאֵינוֹ יוֹדֵעַ לִשְׁאוֹל.

*Ke-neged arba'ah banim dibrah Torah. Eḥad ḥakham, ve-eḥad rasha,
ve-eḥad tam, ve-eḥad she-eino yodei'a lishol.*

The four children can also be different parts of each of us. In fairy tales,
it's easy to figure out who's smart, who's evil, and who's innocent. In
real life, none of us is always wise or always wicked. We change with
our feelings and our knowledge, like prisms that change color with the
slant of sunlight or a ripple of air.

We feel like the wise child when we read and study and ask, "What does
this mean?" about every detail; when we learn how to help ourselves
and respect others; when we know the difference between smart and
smart-alecky.

We feel like the wicked child when we are rowdy or mischievous; when we
doubt our parents or disobey our teachers to get attention; when we are
mean and disrespectful, stamping our feet and shouting, "Who cares!"

We feel like the simple child when we don't understand; when we shake our heads and ask over and over, "What is this all about? Explain it again."

We feel like the child who doesn't know how to ask when we're embarrassed or shy; when we freeze in a new situation and people say, "Cat got your tongue?" Then we feel like slinking into the shadows.

Parents have different sides, too. Sometimes their advice is great. They know just what to do. But when they try to figure out your math homework they feel so simple. If bad things happen in the world that they don't understand, they may not even know how to ask the right questions. When they yell and don't do what you want, you feel like yelling back.

Whatever face of the prism we show, whatever kind of person we are, whatever mood we're in, we're all included at the seder. We can all read and study, question and doubt, listen to the Passover story, and understand its meaning for us.

• Here's a fun way to see different sides of yourself. Take two small mirrors. Hold them up to your face at various angles. Which side do you like best?

וְהִיא שֶׁעָמְדָה
Ve-hi She-amdah
God's Promise

We've already paused in the story to praise God for giving us the Torah. This time we praise God for giving us the strength to survive.

The leader covers the matzot and lifts the wine cup.
Everyone sings together:

וְהִיא שֶׁעָמְדָה לַאֲבוֹתֵינוּ וְלָנוּ, שֶׁלֹּא אֶחָד בִּלְבָד עָמַד עָלֵינוּ לְכַלּוֹתֵנוּ. אֶלָּא שֶׁבְּכָל דּוֹר וָדוֹר עוֹמְדִים עָלֵינוּ לְכַלּוֹתֵנוּ, וְהַקָּדוֹשׁ בָּרוּךְ הוּא מַצִּילֵנוּ מִיָּדָם.

Ve-hi she-amdah l'avoteinu ve-lanu,
She-lo eḥad bil'vad amad aleinu le-khaloteinu.
Ela she-bekhol dor va-dor omdim aleinu le-khaloteinu.
Ve-Ha-Kadosh Barukh Hu matzileinu mi-yadam.

God promised Abraham that his children would become a great nation. In every generation, enemies try to destroy us, but God saves us each time. God keeps the promise.

Enemies. The word spits out bitterness and hatred. It makes us shudder and tremble. Enemies in every generation. Pharaoh, the Egyptian king who whipped our bodies and our spirits. Haman, the Persian adviser who plotted our destruction. Torquemada, Queen Isabella's priest, who in the fifteenth century tormented us and forced us to leave Spain. Hitler, the twentieth-century German leader who tortured, burned, and killed six million Jews. Those who hate us and still want to destroy us today.

But God remembers the promise. Though many of us have suffered and many of us have died, God keeps the Jewish people alive.

The leader puts down the wine cup and uncovers the matzot.

THE STORY OF THE EXODUS
A Play in Four Parts

Finally, the heart of the story!
Go around the table and take turns reading this play, or act it out.

Act I: How we got to Egypt
Act II: What happened to us in Egypt
Act III: What happened when God heard our voices
Act IV: How God took us out of Egypt

Cast of Characters:

Narrator	Yokheved
Abraham	Pharaoh
Jacob	Miriam
Moses	Singers

Act I: How we got to Egypt

Narrator: You know how Grandma and Grandpa like to tell us what life was like before we were born? So the haggadah is going to tell us what life was like before the Jewish people was born.

Abraham: Shalom. I'm Abraham. I'm known as the father of the Jewish people. A long, long time ago, I was living peacefully in the land of Ur Kasdim. Suddenly I heard God calling me to leave. I'd never heard a Voice like that before, so I took my wife Sarah, my nephew Lot, all my camels and donkeys and everything else I owned, and I left. I traveled to the land of Canaan, which is now Israel.

One night I had a strange yearning to go for a walk under the stars. As I was walking, the Voice said to me, "Abraham, do you see those stars? That's how many people your family will grow to have." I thought that was a funny promise, because I didn't even have one child yet. But a few years later, I had a child named Isaac, and he had a child named Jacob. God had kept the first part of the promise.

Narrator: The Torah tells us:

אֲרַמִּי אֹבֵד אָבִי, וַיֵּרֶד מִצְרַיְמָה, וַיָּגָר שָׁם בִּמְתֵי מְעָט.
וַיְהִי שָׁם לְגוֹי גָּדוֹל, עָצוּם וָרָב.

Arami oved avi, va-yered Mitzraymah, va-yagor sham bi-m'tei me'at.
Va-yehi sham le-goy gadol, atzum va-rav.

My father, Jacob, fled to Egypt and settled there. From his small family grew a great nation.

Jacob: I'm Jacob, the guy who moved to Egypt. After I married Rachel and Leah and had lots of children, I escaped from the clutches of my mean father-in-law, Laban, who also happened to be my uncle. We settled down in Canaan, where we lived a good life. But then a terrible famine began. There was no wheat or barley anywhere! And I had twelve children to feed! I used to have thirteen, but my poor Joseph—my favorite son—was eaten by a wild animal. At least that's what his brothers told me. I heard that the storehouses in Egypt were overflowing with food, so I sent my sons there to buy some grain.

Would you believe the Egyptian leader they met in Egypt was none other than Joseph? Those sons of mine had fibbed to me. They were so jealous of Joseph that they had actually sold him to a band of Midianites, who sold him again to Potiphar the Egyptian. When Pharaoh—that's the name all the rulers of Egypt used—had some bad dreams, Joseph interpreted them correctly. He saved all of Egypt from going hungry. Joseph became a very important person and invited the whole family—all seventy of us, plus our sheep and goats and chickens—to move from Canaan to Egypt. I wasn't sure it was a good idea, but then I heard the Voice. God said not to be afraid and promised we would still become a great nation. So we went! The land of Goshen became our new home.

Singers:
(To the tune of *Yankee Doodle*)

Jacob's family packed their bags
To flee from Uncle Laban,
They headed back to Canaan land,
A safe and lovely haven.

Then a famine hit the land,
No water and no grain,
So Jacob said, "To Egypt go,
My sons, do not complain."

Chorus:
Later Jacob got the word
That Joseph did survive.
In Egypt, second in command,
He kept the land alive.

In Goshen they did build their homes,
They soon increased their power.
They offered grateful thanks to God
Who brought them to this hour.

Chorus:
Jacob's clan then tilled the land.
In Goshen life was charming,
Until mean Pharaoh came along,
His cruelty was alarming.

Can you guess who this is?
Hint: He was Pharaoh's second in command.

Act II: What happened to us in Egypt

Narrator: The Torah tells us:

וַיָּרֵעוּ אֹתָנוּ הַמִּצְרִים וַיְעַנּוּנוּ, וַיִּתְּנוּ עָלֵינוּ עֲבֹדָה קָשָׁה.

Va-yare'u otanu ha-Mitzrim va-y'a'nunu, va-yitnu aleinu avodah kashah.

The Egyptians treated us harshly and made us work very hard.

Moses: I'm Moses. I grow up to be the leader who takes the Jewish people out of Egypt. Too bad not all Pharaohs are alike. The Pharaoh who was so kind to Joseph and Jacob died, and suddenly everything changed for our family. My mom, Yokheved, told me that the new Pharaoh was afraid our family was growing too fast and getting too strong. Pharaoh decided to put all my uncles and cousins and brothers to work as slaves, building cities to glorify him. He didn't want us to survive, so he ordered that all newborn baby boys should be thrown into the Nile River. Maybe he ignored the baby girls because he thought girls couldn't grow up to be strong and work hard. Little did he know how important women would be to the Passover story. . . .

Yokheved: Hooray for the girls and the women! I'm Yokheved, Moses' mom. From the minute he was born, I knew Moses was something special. I knew I had to save him. So I put him in a basket that floated on the river, and told my daughter, Miriam, to watch over him. Soon she ran back and told me that Pharaoh's daughter had found the basket and fell in love with the baby. Miriam was so clever that she arranged for me to nurse Moses until he was grown up enough to move into Pharaoh's palace.

Moses: I lived a life of luxury in the palace, but I never quite fit in. One day I saw how harshly the Egyptian taskmasters were treating the Hebrew slaves. I got so mad! I hit one of the taskmasters and killed him. I didn't think anyone saw me, but I couldn't be sure. I ran away to the land of Midian, met my wife, Tzipporah, and became a shepherd.

Singers:
(To the tune of *Sing a Song of Sixpence*)

Sing a song of Yokheved,
A good and faithful wife,
She was growing tired of
A most unbearable life.
Moses in a basket,
She put her newborn son,
Until the Pharaoh's daughter came
And saved the little one.

"Living in the palace
Far away from me,
Moses didn't realize
His people's slavery.
Still I saw him daily
Appointed as his nurse,
I pray he'll grow so proud and strong
To lift the Pharaoh's curse."

One day in the mud fields
Moses walked about,
Looked upon an Israelite
Beaten inside out,
To the Egyptian taskman, cruel to the slave,
He spoke with anger and he said,
"That's not how we behave!"

Act III: What happened when God heard our voices

Narrator: The Torah tells us:

וַנִּצְעַק אֶל יהוה אֱלֹהֵי אֲבֹתֵינוּ, וַיִּשְׁמַע יהוה אֶת קֹלֵנוּ, וַיַּרְא אֶת עָנְיֵנוּ וְאֶת עֲמָלֵנוּ וְאֶת לַחֲצֵנוּ.

Va-nitz'ak el Adonai elohei avoteinu, va-yishma Adonai et koleinu, va-yar et onyeinu ve-et amaleinu ve-et laḥatzeinu.

We cried out to God. God heard our voices and saw our suffering.

Moses: It was nice and quiet in Midian. But what I had seen in Egypt still bothered me. I wondered if it bothered anyone else. One day I followed a little lamb that had wandered away from my flock. As I climbed up Mount Ḥoreb, I rubbed my eyes in disbelief. I saw a burning bush crackling with fire, but its leaves were still green and unharmed! From the bush I heard a Voice that said:

"Go down, Moses,
Way down in Egypt land.
Tell old Pharaoh,
To let my people go!"

Moses: What would you have done? I was scared. I tried to make excuses. I said I wasn't a good public speaker, that I stuttered and I was terrible with crowds. I said no one would listen to me. I didn't even have a sword or a spear to frighten people into listening. "God," I pleaded, "choose someone else." Of course, God—the Voice—had all the answers. God said my brother, Aaron, would help me speak, and that God would give me powerful signs so Pharaoh and the Israelites would believe me. What could I do? I went back to Egypt and, together with Aaron, faced Pharaoh at the palace.

Singers:
(To the tune of *B-I-N-G-O*)

There was a man named Moses, and
freedom was his aim-oh!

Let my people go,
Egypt, our evil foe.
No more tears should flow.
So let my people go!

There was a stubborn-hearted king,
And his name was Pharaoh.

No, no, you will not go—
You will bow so low.
Oh, no, you will not go—
Instead your work will grow!

Act IV: How God took us out of Egypt

Narrator: The Torah tells us:

וַיּוֹצִיאֵנוּ יהוה מִמִּצְרַיִם בְּיָד חֲזָקָה וּבִזְרוֹעַ נְטוּיָה, וּבְמֹרָא גָּדֹל וּבְאֹתוֹת וּבְמֹפְתִים.

Va-yotzi'einu Adonai mi-Mitzrayim be-yad ḥazakah u-vi-zro'a netuyah, u-v'mora gadol u-v'otot u-v'moftim.

God took us out of Egypt with a strong hand, an outstretched arm, and with signs and wonders.

Pharaoh: I didn't pay much attention to Moses until I felt the hand of this power he called God. First Moses' wooden stick turned into a snake, but my magicians matched Moses' and Aaron's hocus-pocus. Then Moses and Aaron said God would bring ten plagues on Egypt. First the Nile River turned red with blood. Next, slimy green frogs hopped in my bed, on my head, and all over Egypt. We lived through seven more plagues: lice, wild beasts, cattle disease, boils, hail, locusts, and darkness. And while we suffered, the Israelites were spared! Moses said God passed over their houses during each plague. Finally, all our firstborn sons died during the tenth plague. I'd had enough!

Singers:
(To the tune of *Three Blind Mice*)

Blood and frogs,
Lice and beasts,
Boils and hail,
Cattle disease,
Bugs that feasted on all our land,
Darkness so thick that it's hard to stand
Our firstborn dead—that's not what we planned.
The ten bad plagues.
Ten bad plagues.

Pharaoh: "Go!" I said to Moses and Aaron. "I never want to see you again!"

Moses: God saved us! We would soon be free! We packed our few belongings in a hurry, baked a little matzah, and streamed out of Egypt—all 600,000 of us! How our numbers had grown since Jacob first brought us to Egypt!

Narrator: And just when things were looking good . . . .

Pharaoh (interrupting): Wait a minute. I think I miss those slaves already. I'd grown accustomed to their faces—and their hard work. I'm going to call my chariots, chase them, and bring them back.

Miriam: I'm Miriam, Moses' and Aaron's sister. I believe in what God and my brothers have done. But now I'm really scared. We're at the Red Sea, and Pharaoh's chariots are hot on our heels. Where will we go? (*Gasps*) Wow! The waters are parting! We can walk right through on dry land. What a miracle God has created. Will Pharaoh be able to follow us through? No! The waters are closing over the Egyptian chariots! God parted the waters just for us. We're safe. We're free. I feel like singing to God for saving us and making us into a great nation!

Singers: *Miriam's Song*

Chorus:
And the women dancing with their timbrels
Followed Miriam as she sang her song,
Sing a song to the One whom we've exalted,
Miriam and the women danced and danced the whole night long.

When Miriam stood upon the shores and gazed across the sea
The wonder of this miracle she soon came to believe
Whoever thought the sea would part with an outstretched hand
And we would pass to freedom and march to the promised land.

Everyone (bowing): The end!

Miriam's Song

Music and Lyrics: Debbie Friedman
Based on Exodus 15: 20–21

עֶשֶׂר מַכּוֹת
Eser Makkot
The Ten Plagues

The play is over, but the Ten Plagues require a story all their own. . . .

I remember standing on the shore of the Red Sea,
the waves churning upright,
solid walls of water.
You embraced me as the last Israelite child crossed over safely,
and we sank to the ground to praise God.
But then we heard the hoofbeats of the Egyptian horses,
the clank and clatter of their chariots.
We raised our heads in fear,
and suddenly—
Whoosh!

The water crashed down with a roar,
and all that was left of our enemies were
wheels and helmets and feathery plumes
floating in the water.
We sank down again and cried
in happiness and sadness.

In the Talmud, a book of Jewish law and teachings written by rabbis long ago, a story teaches us: While the Egyptians were drowning in the sea, the angels in heaven began to sing praises to God. God silenced them. "How can you sing?" God asked, "while My children are drowning?"

We spill ten drops of wine from our cups to show that just as our cups should not be totally full, so our hearts should not be full. We cannot be completely happy, because people died in order for us to become free.

Dip a pinky or index finger in the wine and spill out a drop onto a plate as you recite the name of each plague.

אֵלוּ עֶשֶׂר מַכּוֹת שֶׁהֵבִיא הַקָּדוֹשׁ בָּרוּךְ הוּא עַל הַמִּצְרִים בְּמִצְרָיִם. וְאֵלוּ הֵן:

Elu eser makkot she-heivi Ha-Kadosh Barukh Hu al ha-Mitzrim be-Mitzrayim. Ve-elu hen:

Blood	Dam	דָּם
Frogs	Tzefarde'a	צְפַרְדֵּעַ
Lice	Kinim	כִּנִּים
Wild Beasts	Arov	עָרוֹב
Cattle Disease	Dever	דֶּבֶר
Boils	Shehin	שְׁחִין
Hail	Barad	בָּרָד
Locusts	Arbeh	אַרְבֶּה
Darkness	Hoshekh	חֹשֶׁךְ
Death of the Firstborn	Makkat Bekhorot	מַכַּת בְּכוֹרוֹת

Plagues are not always punishments. Today, bad things also "plague" the world: water and air pollution, animals facing extinction, AIDS, cancer, COVID, and other diseases.

• Let's take scallions, or anything else with an unpleasant smell, and beat them against the table as we recite the names of the new plagues in our world today.

That's what Jews from Iran do when they recite *Dayyenu*, the next section of the haggadah. They take long bunches of scallions or leeks—vegetables that have an oniony smell—and beat each other lightly on the back and shoulders to feel as if they were still in Egypt, when the taskmaster wielded his whip. How can we help to rid the world of these plagues?

דַּיֵּנוּ

Dayyenu
That Would Have Been Enough

Picture a box tied with a beautiful bow. Open it. . . .
It's a present you've been dreaming of!
Wait . . . there's more inside: Another box with a second gift.
"How many kindnesses you show me!" you say.
Inside the second gift there's a third.
"This is beyond my hopes!" you exclaim.
Inside the third gift there's a fourth, and then a fifth—a whole series of
gifts. "If you had given me just one gift," you say, shaking your head
in disbelief, "that would have been enough. But for all these gifts I say,
thank you."

אִלּוּ הוֹצִיאָנוּ מִמִּצְרַיִם,　דַּיֵּנוּ:
אִלּוּ נָתַן לָנוּ אֶת הַשַּׁבָּת,　דַּיֵּנוּ:
אִלּוּ נָתַן לָנוּ אֶת הַתּוֹרָה,　דַּיֵּנוּ.

Ilu hotzi'anu mi-Mitzrayim, dayyenu.
Ilu natan lanu et ha-Shabbat, dayyenu.
Ilu natan lanu et ha-Torah, dayyenu.

On Passover we remember the many gifts God has given us. If God had
just taken us out of Egypt and given us the gift of freedom we'd been
dreaming of, that would have been enough. *Dayyenu.*

If God had led us across the Red Sea and hadn't taken care of us in the
desert for forty years, that would have been enough. *Dayyenu.*

If God had given us Shabbat without giving us the Torah, that would
have been enough. *Dayyenu.*

If God had given us the Torah and hadn't led us to the land of Israel, that would have been enough. *Dayyenu*.

But God gave us all these gifts and more. And for that we say, thank you!

• Take an empty box and pretend it's a beautiful present. Now open it. Some of the gifts God has given *you* are inside. What would you find?

שְׁלֹשָׁה סְמָנִים שֶׁל פֶּסַח
Pesaḥ, Matzah, Maror
The Three Passover Symbols

Rabbi Gamliel, a great teacher and scholar
who lived almost two thousand years ago,
helped create the Passover seder.
No seder is complete, he said,
unless it includes an explanation of three symbols:
Pesaḥ, *matzah*, and *maror*.

רַבָּן גַּמְלִיאֵל הָיָה אוֹמֵר: כָּל שֶׁלֹּא אָמַר שְׁלֹשָׁה דְבָרִים אֵלּוּ בַּפֶּסַח לֹא יָצָא יְדֵי
חוֹבָתוֹ, וְאֵלּוּ הֵן: פֶּסַח, מַצָּה, וּמָרוֹר.

Rabban Gamliel hayah omer:
Kol she-lo amar sh'loshah devarim elu ba-Pesaḥ
lo yatza y'dei ḥovato,
Ve-elu hen: Pesaḥ, matzah, u-maror.

Take turns reciting each of the following explanations of the three
symbols, or say them together.

Everyone points to the zero'a, the roasted bone.
Pesaḥ, the roasted bone, reminds us that God "passed over" (*pasaḥ*)
the homes of the Israelites and spared them from the plagues.

The leader lifts the matzah.
Matzah reminds us that the Israelites left Egypt in such a hurry,
even the dough didn't have time to rise.

The leader lifts the maror.
Maror reminds us how bitter the Egyptians made our lives in slavery.

I heard the cries of the Egyptians—
mothers and fathers mourning their firstborn children.
They kept me awake all night.
We had smeared the blood of a lamb on our doorpost
so God would "pass over" our home.
As I readied the dough for our trip,
I prayed God would free us from the bitterness of our lives.
"Bake that dough the way it is," you cried to me suddenly.
"There's no time to delay."
As I watched the dough harden quickly over the fire,
a firm hope leapt up through the flame.
"Be strong and have courage," it called to me.
I knew slavery had not defeated us.

• The Israelites only had a few moments to gather their belongings.
Picture yourself packing your own backpack alongside them. Fill
it with everything you would take if you were leaving Egypt.

בְּכָל דּוֹר וָדוֹר
Bekhol Dor Va-Dor
In Every Generation

In every generation we should feel as if we ourselves had left Egypt. Even though we live long after the exodus from Egypt, we must picture ourselves fleeing slavery.

בְּכָל דּוֹר וָדוֹר חַיָּב אָדָם לִרְאוֹת אֶת עַצְמוֹ כְּאִלּוּ הוּא יָצָא מִמִּצְרָיִם.

Be-khol dor va-dor ḥayav adam lir'ot et atzmo ke-ilu hu yatza mi-Mitzrayim.

Different Jewish communities have creative ways of imagining themselves in Egypt. Jews from India tie some matzah in a sack. A child puts it on his shoulder. The parent asks the child: "From where have you come?" "*Mi-Mitzrayim*," answers the child. "From Egypt." "Where are you going?" "*L'Yerushalayim*. To Jerusalem." "What are you taking with you?" The child points to the sack of matzah.

We can never take freedom for granted. Slavery did not end when we left Egypt. It continued into other times when we were forbidden to practice our religion. It continues today.

The Beta Israel, Jews from Ethiopia, escaped from danger in the recent past. They were feared and hated by their Ethiopian neighbors, but they refused to give up the Jewish traditions. Many were kidnapped and sold as slaves. Villages were burned to the ground. Though the Beta Israel were forbidden to leave Ethiopia, they tied up their few belongings, packed bread, dried meat, and chickpeas, and trekked by night across mountains and deserts—hundreds of miles by foot. Then they boarded planes provided secretly by the Israeli government that took them to the land of Israel. Nearly ten thousand Beta Israel were rescued in the first secret airlift, Operation Moses, and fourteen thousand more during a second airlift, Operation Solomon.

• Imagine leaving Egypt, Ethiopia, or any other place of danger as you act out the words of this song.

Out of Egypt

No time to linger
Get out of bed.
Put on your sandals
Cover your head.
Roll up the blankets
Tie up the sack.
This on your shoulder
That one on your back.

Chorus: Out, out of Egypt to be free! *(2x)*

No time to bake now
Just take the dough.
Water, take water
Keep voices low.
Pick up the baby
Hold sister's hand.
Come follow Moses
To the Promised Land.

Chorus: Out, out of Egypt to be free! *(2x)*

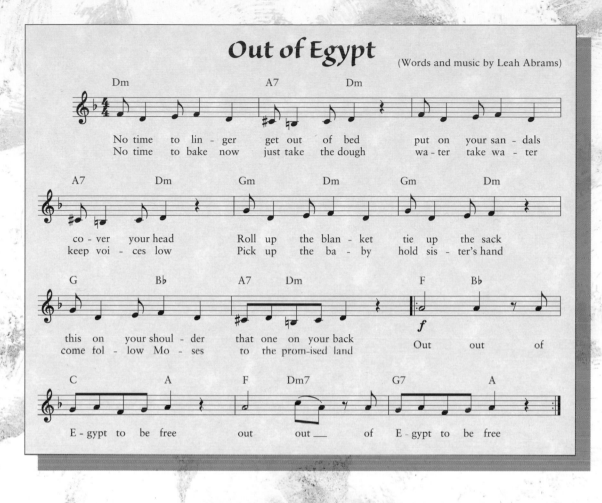

Out of Egypt

(Words and music by Leah Abrams)

הַלְלוּיָה
Halleluyah

When we were slaves,
our song to God was made of sighs.
Its melody flowed with tears.
Its words echoed our cries.
Now that we're free,
we sing a new song to God,
a soaring song of celebration.
Its melody flows with joy.
Its words echo our elation.

וְנֹאמַר לְפָנָיו שִׁירָה חֲדָשָׁה. הַלְלוּיָה.

Ve-nomar lefanav shirah ḥadashah. Halleluyah.

Let us sing a new song to God. Halleluyah.

Ve-nomar Lefanav

Joyously   Hassidic

Ve - no-mar le-fa - nav shi-rah ḥa-da - shah ve-no-mar le-fa - nav

shi-rah ḥa-da-shah ve-shi-rah ḥa-da-shah ha - le-lu - yah

ha - le-lu - yah ha - le-lu - yah ha-le-lu - yah ha-le-lu - yah

כּוֹס שֵׁנִי
Kos Sheni
The Second Cup

The leader lifts the second cup of wine and says:

בָּרוּךְ אַתָּה יהוה גָּאַל יִשְׂרָאֵל.

Barukh atah Adonai, ga'al Yisrael.

Praised are You, Adonai our God, Who saved Israel.

בָּרוּךְ אַתָּה יהוה אֱלֹהֵינוּ מֶלֶךְ הָעוֹלָם, בּוֹרֵא פְּרִי הַגָּפֶן.

Barukh atah Adonai eloheinu melekh ha-olam, borei p'ri ha-gafen.

Praised are You, Adonai our God, Ruler of the universe, Who creates the fruit of the vine.

Drink the second cup of wine, leaning to the left.

רָחְצָה
Roḥtzah
Wash the Hands a Second Time

We've talked and asked, explained and discussed, and finally, it's time to eat! Before we do, we wash our hands, that cool tickle of water reminding us again that food is one of God's many blessings. This time, we bless God, too.

Pass around a pitcher of water, a bowl, and towel. Hold the pitcher in one hand and pour water over the other hand. Reverse hands and repeat. Dry your hands and recite:

בָּרוּךְ אַתָּה יהוה אֱלֹהֵינוּ מֶלֶךְ הָעוֹלָם, אֲשֶׁר קִדְּשָׁנוּ בְּמִצְוֹתָיו וְצִוָּנוּ עַל נְטִילַת יָדָיִם.

*Barukh atah Adonai eloheinu melekh ha-olam,
asher kid'shanu be-mitzvotav ve-tzivanu al netilat yadayim.*

Praised are You, Adonai our God, Ruler of the universe, Who has commanded us to cleanse our hands.

מוֹצִיא מַצָּה
Motzi/Matzah
Eat the Matzah

Read silently:

Between the time we wash our hands and make the blessing over the matzah, it's a tradition not to speak, not to interrupt the two small actions that together make one large action.

In the silence we can hear the story we've just told and the songs we've just sung, the crack of the taskmaster's whip and the *ribbet, ribbet* of frogs. We can hear God's voice through the burning bush, Miriam's song at the Red Sea, and the stamping of the Israelites' marching feet. We can hear the anxious calls of the Israelites as they fled, and the crunch of the matzah they baked—the same matzah we eat in remembrance today.

Who can wait to taste the matzah? Once a sign of slavery, it is now a symbol of freedom. We take two matzot—the very top matzah and the broken middle matzah—to remember the food called manna the Israelites ate every day of the forty years they wandered in the desert.

Manna was a magical food that fell in a fine layer with the dew each morning. It looked like a little seed, the color of crystal or pearl, but when it was ground and baked, it tasted like a cake dipped in honey or a rich dough. Every day the Israelites went out to collect manna. On Friday God gave them a double amount of manna so they would have enough for that day and the next—Shabbat, a time for rest.

The leader recites the following two blessings aloud,
then gives a piece of each of the top two matzot to every person.

בָּרוּךְ אַתָּה יהוה אֱלֹהֵינוּ מֶלֶךְ הָעוֹלָם, הַמוֹצִיא לֶחֶם מִן הָאָרֶץ.

Barukh atah Adonai eloheinu melekh ha-olam,
ha-motzi leḥem min ha-aretz.

Praised are You, Adonai our God, Ruler of the universe,
Who brings forth bread from the earth.

בָּרוּךְ אַתָּה יהוה אֱלֹהֵינוּ מֶלֶךְ הָעוֹלָם, אֲשֶׁר קִדְּשָׁנוּ בְּמִצְוֹתָיו וְצִוָּנוּ
עַל אֲכִילַת מַצָּה.

Barukh atah Adonai eloheinu melekh ha-olam
asher kid'shanu be-mitzvotav ve-tzivanu al akhilat matzah.

Praised are You, Adonai our God, Ruler of the universe,
Who has commanded us to eat the matzah.

מָרוֹר
Maror
Eat the Bitter Herbs

The pungent taste of *maror* reminds us of the bitterness of cruelty and oppression. No time in recent history has been more bitter for the Jewish people than the Holocaust, when the Nazis in Germany and Eastern Europe killed six million Jews and five million other people. The Nazis believed that people who were different from them should be destroyed. They especially hated the Jewish people and blamed them for many of Germany's problems. They rounded people up and put them in concentration camps, where millions suffered and millions died.

Amidst the death and despair, some Jews during the Holocaust still remembered the Jewish holidays. They still wanted to observe the Passover laws, though they had no wine, no matzah, no *ḥaroset*, no real *maror*—just the bitterness of hatred. While some lost their faith in God, many continued to believe that they would be freed.

Here is part of a poem written by Elie Wiesel, who survived the Holocaust and became a spokesman for thousands of other survivors.

It is night,
The first night of Passover.
The camp is asleep.
He alone is awake.
He talks to himself
Soundlessly.
I hear his words,
I capture his silence.
To himself, to me,
He is saying:
I have not partaken of matzoth,
Nor of marror.

I have not emptied the four cups,
Symbols of the four deliverances.
I did not invite
The hungry
To share my repast—
Or even my hunger.
No longer have I a son
To ask me
The four questions—
No longer have I the strength
To answer.
(From *Ani Ma'amin, A Song Lost and Found Again*)

Despite his suffering during the Holocaust, Elie Wiesel found hope and faith. He grew up, married, and had a son, Elisha. Elie Wiesel became a famous Jewish writer and won the Nobel Peace Prize for his work on behalf of the rights of Jews and for the freedom of human beings everywhere.

Dip the *maror* into the *ḥaroset*, a symbol of the mortar and bricks of Egypt but also of hope and sweetness. The bitterness of slavery can be sweetened with the hope of freedom.

Recite the blessing before eating the maror:

בָּרוּךְ אַתָּה יהוה אֱלֹהֵינוּ מֶלֶךְ הָעוֹלָם, אֲשֶׁר קִדְּשָׁנוּ בְּמִצְוֹתָיו וְצִוָּנוּ
עַל אֲכִילַת מָרוֹר.

Barukh atah Adonai eloheinu melekh ha-olam,
asher kid'shanu be-mitzvotav ve-tzivanu al akhilat maror.

Praised are You, Adonai our God, Ruler of the universe,
Who has commanded us to eat *maror.*

כּוֹרֵךְ
Korekh
Eat the Hillel Sandwich

We don't dwell on sadness at the seder. After *maror*, we move on.

Make up a recipe for a funny sandwich. Raisins and mayonnaise on rye bread? Strawberries, lettuce, and chips between two slices of cheese? Peanut butter and carrot strips on a bagel?

On Passover, God told us we should eat three special foods together: roasted lamb, matzah, and *maror*. Rabbi Hillel turned God's instructions into a recipe for an unusual sandwich. Between two pieces of matzah, put *maror* and roasted lamb from the Passover sacrifice. When the Temple in Jerusalem was destroyed and there were no more sacrifices, we stopped using the roasted lamb in the Hillel sandwich.

Each person takes two pieces of the bottom matzah. Put horseradish or romaine lettuce in between. Some people dip the sandwich in ḥaroset. We recall Rabbi Hillel's sandwich as we say:

זֵכֶר לְמִקְדָּשׁ כְּהִלֵּל. כֵּן עָשָׂה הִלֵּל בִּזְמַן שֶׁבֵּית הַמִּקְדָּשׁ הָיָה קַיָּם. הָיָה כּוֹרֵךְ פֶּסַח מַצָּה וּמָרוֹר וְאוֹכֵל בְּיַחַד, לְקַיֵּם מַה שֶׁנֶּאֱמַר: עַל מַצּוֹת וּמְרֹרִים יֹאכְלֻהוּ.

Zekher le-mikdash ke-Hillel. Ken asah Hillel bi-z'man she-beit ha-mikdash hayah kayam. Hayah korekh pesaḥ, matzah, u-maror ve-okhel be-yaḥad, le-kayem mah she-ne'emar: al matzot u-m'rorim yokh'luhu.

Eat the sandwich, leaning to the left.

שֻׁלְחָן עוֹרֵךְ
Shulḥan Orekh
Enjoy the Meal

Make way for a mouth-watering feast of golden chicken soup and fluffy matzah balls; roasted chicken, spicy vegetable stews, and crisp cold salads; fruity matzah and potato puddings; macaroons, chocolates, nut cakes, and candies. The Passover feast is a *se'udat mitzvah*, a meal that accompanies a religious celebration. Like a card you make more special by decorating it with neon markers and glitter, so we make the seder more special with a festive meal of delicious foods.

Here are two sample menus:

A TRADITIONAL ASHKENAZIC MENU
Chicken soup with matzah balls
Chicken cutlets
Roasted potatoes
Apple-raisin-farfel pudding
Green salad
Chocolate chip cookies
Fruit

A SEPHARDIC VEGETARIAN MENU
Eggplant or Spinach *Mina* (layered casserole)
Vegan Stuffed Acorn Squash
Indian-Spiced Curried Vegetables
Herbed Quinoa Pilaf
Israeli Salad
Mango and Papaya with mint
Tishpishti: Turkish Nut Cake Soaked in Orange Blossom Syrup

Seder Meal Recipes

Ask a grown-up to help with cutting, chopping, and using the oven.

Chicken Cutlets

8 chicken cutlets
1/2 cup matzah meal
1/2 teaspoon salt
1/2 teaspoon paprika
2 tablespoons fresh parsley, chopped,
  or 1 tablespoon dried parsley
1–2 tablespoons vegetable oil

Preheat oven to 350°. Combine all ingredients in a wide bowl except chicken and oil. Dip chicken into the matzah meal mixture to coat it. Place coated cutlets in single layer on a baking pan. Dribble oil over tops of cutlets. Bake uncovered 45 minutes or until chicken is white inside.

Vegetarian Matzah Kugel

1 head fresh broccoli, broken into small pieces and steamed,
   or 1 package frozen broccoli, cooked
1 tablespoon oil
1 onion, diced
1/2 stalk celery, diced
1/2 pound mushrooms, sliced
1 clove garlic, pressed or chopped
2 tablespoons chopped parsley
2 tablespoons chopped dill
1/2 teaspoon salt
1/2 teaspoon paprika
2 1/2 cups matzah farfel
1 cup boiling water
4 eggs, beaten
1 teaspoon prepared soup mix or 1 bouillon cube

Preheat oven to 350°. Place farfel in colander. Pour boiling water over farfel and drain. Sauté onion and celery in oil until translucent. Add mushrooms and cook another few minutes until the mushrooms are soft. Combine the farfel with the vegetables, add the rest of the ingredients—except the paprika—and mix well. Turn into a 9 x 13–inch baking dish. Sprinkle the top with paprika. Bake 1/2 hour until firm.

Tishpishti: Turkish Nut Cake

5 eggs, lightly beaten
1 1/4 cups walnuts, chopped
3/4 cup ground almonds
1 cup sugar
Juice and grated zest of 1 orange
2 teaspoons cinnamon

For the syrup:
2 1/4 cups sugar
2 cups water
1 tablespoon lemon juice
1 tablespoon rose water

Make the syrup first, so that it has time to chill. Boil the sugar and water with the lemon juice for 10-15 minutes. Stir in the rose water. Let it cool, then put in the refrigerator.

Mix all the cake ingredients thoroughly. Line the bottom of a cake pan with foil or greaseproof paper. Brush the foil and the sides of the tin with oil and pour the cake mixture in. Bake in a preheated 350° oven for 1 hour, until browned. Turn cake out upside down onto a deep serving dish as soon as it is out of the oven. Peel off the foil, cut into serving pieces, and pour the cold syrup all over the hot cake. After 1/2 hour, turn the pieces over so that they can thoroughly absorb the syrup.

As we enjoy so much delicious food, let's remember those who are not as lucky as we are.

• You may want to donate food, money, or your time to an organization that feeds hungry people. Here are some ideas:
- •Met Council on Jewish Poverty, New York: metcouncil.org
- •Jewish Family Service LA: jfsla.org/our-services/food-hunger/
- •Leket Israel, Israel's national food bank: leket.org/en/

Searching for something local?
- •Look for a nearby soup kitchen
- •Find a community garden that donates their produce

צָפוּן
Tzafun
Find and Eat the Afikoman

Ready, get set, go! It's time to find that *afikoman*! We've spied out the territory and mapped out our plan. But what's the treasure we're trying so hard to find? A piece of broken matzah?

We journeyed for days until we reached the foot of a mountain.
Mount Sinai.
My feet were sore and I was so hungry,
I even missed the onions and garlic we ate in Egypt.
We searched our knapsacks and pockets for a bit of food,
but our hands came out empty.
We searched Grandfather's tent and Mother's bundles,
Father's robe and Uncle's cap.
We even looked for crumbs in our lambs' woolly coats.
Nothing.
But when we turned over Grandmother's kneading trough,
we got lucky!
A broken piece of matzah was stuck inside!
We shared it, and it tasted of creamy milk and fresh honey.
It tasted of freedom.
We agreed not to eat the last tiny piece.
We broke it in half, wrapped the pieces in two long pieces of cloth,
and dangled them from our necks like the most precious jewelry.
"To bring us good luck on the rest of our journey!" you said with a smile.
"Do you know what we've found?" I asked. "A treasure!"

Today we still hunt for the treasures hiding inside us and around us. Freedom. Peace. Kindness. Hope. As we work toward those big treasures, enjoy the small prizes you may receive for finding the *afikoman*.

The leader passes out pieces of the afikoman. *Eat it, leaning to the left. Enjoy the last bite, because we don't eat anything else for the rest of the seder.*

בָּרֵךְ

Barekh
Recite the Blessings After the Meal

From the time we were small, our parents have taught us to say, "Thank you." God has given us the gift of food and now, with our stomachs full of matzah balls and macaroons, we say "thank you" by reciting *Birkat Ha-mazon*, the blessings after the meal.

We thank God for giving food to all living things and for giving us the land of Israel. We ask God for the blessings of life, health, and peace, and for a rebuilt Jerusalem. We praise God for all that's good.

Everybody sings together:

בָּרוּךְ אַתָּה יהוה אֱלֹהֵינוּ מֶלֶךְ הָעוֹלָם, הַזָּן אֶת הָעוֹלָם כֻּלּוֹ בְּטוּבוֹ, בְּחֵן בְּחֶסֶד וּבְרַחֲמִים. הוּא נוֹתֵן לֶחֶם לְכָל בָּשָׂר כִּי לְעוֹלָם חַסְדּוֹ. וּבְטוּבוֹ הַגָּדוֹל תָּמִיד לֹא חָסַר לָנוּ, וְאַל יֶחְסַר לָנוּ מָזוֹן לְעוֹלָם וָעֶד, בַּעֲבוּר שְׁמוֹ הַגָּדוֹל, כִּי הוּא אֵל זָן וּמְפַרְנֵס לַכֹּל, וּמֵטִיב לַכֹּל וּמֵכִין מָזוֹן לְכָל בְּרִיּוֹתָיו אֲשֶׁר בָּרָא. בָּרוּךְ אַתָּה יהוה, הַזָּן אֶת הַכֹּל.

Barukh atah Adonai eloheinu melekh ha-olam, ha-zan et ha-olam kulo be-tuvo, be-ḥen be-ḥesed u-v'raḥamim. Hu noten leḥem le-khol basar ki le-olam ḥasdo. U-v'tuvo ha-gadol tamid lo ḥasar lanu ve-al yeḥsar lanu mazon le-olam va-ed, ba'avur shemo ha-gadol, ki hu el zan u-m'farnes la-kol, u-metiv la-kol u-mekhin mazon le-khol b'riyotav asher bara. Barukh atah Adonai, ha-zan et ha-kol.

נוֹדֶה לְךָ יהוה אֱלֹהֵינוּ עַל שֶׁהִנְחַלְתָּ לַאֲבוֹתֵינוּ אֶרֶץ חֶמְדָּה טוֹבָה וּרְחָבָה, בְּרִית וְתוֹרָה, חַיִּים וּמָזוֹן. יִתְבָּרַךְ שִׁמְךָ בְּפִי כָּל חַי תָּמִיד לְעוֹלָם וָעֶד, כַּכָּתוּב: וְאָכַלְתָּ וְשָׂבָעְתָּ וּבֵרַכְתָּ אֶת יהוה אֱלֹהֶיךָ עַל הָאָרֶץ הַטֹּבָה אֲשֶׁר נָתַן לָךְ. בָּרוּךְ אַתָּה יהוה, עַל הָאָרֶץ וְעַל הַמָּזוֹן.

Nodeh l'kha Adonai eloheinu al she-hinhalta l'avoteinu eretz hemdah
tovah u-r'havah, b'rit ve-Torah, hayyim u-mazon. Yitbarakh shimkha
be-fi kol hai tamid le-olam va-ed. Ka-katuv: ve-akhalta ve-savata
u-verakhta et Adonai elohekha al ha-aretz ha-tovah asher natan lakh.
Barukh atah Adonai, al ha-aretz ve-al ha-mazon.

וּבְנֵה יְרוּשָׁלַיִם עִיר הַקֹּדֶשׁ בִּמְהֵרָה בְיָמֵינוּ. בָּרוּךְ אַתָּה יהוה, בּוֹנֵה בְּרַחֲמָיו
יְרוּשָׁלָיִם. אָמֵן.

U-v'nei Yerushalayim ir ha-kodesh bi-m'herah ve-yameinu.
Barukh atah Adonai, boneh ve-rahamav Yerushalayim. Amen.

בָּרוּךְ אַתָּה יהוה אֱלֹהֵינוּ מֶלֶךְ הָעוֹלָם, הַמֶּלֶךְ הַטּוֹב וְהַמֵּטִיב לַכֹּל. הוּא הֵטִיב,
הוּא מֵטִיב, הוּא יֵיטִיב לָנוּ. הוּא גְמָלָנוּ הוּא גוֹמְלֵנוּ הוּא יִגְמְלֵנוּ לָעַד, חֵן וָחֶסֶד
וְרַחֲמִים, וִיזַכֵּנוּ לִימוֹת הַמָּשִׁיחַ.

Barukh atah Adonai eloheinu melekh ha-olam,
ha-melekh ha-tov ve-ha-metiv la-kol,
Hu hetiv, hu metiv, hu yeitiv lanu.
Hu g'malanu hu gom'lenu hu yig'm'lenu la'ad,
hen va-hesed ve-rahamim, vi-zakenu limot ha-mashiah.

הָרַחֲמָן הוּא יַנְחִילֵנוּ יוֹם שֶׁכֻּלוֹ טוֹב.

Ha-rahaman, hu yanhileinu yom she-kulo tov.

עֹשֶׂה שָׁלוֹם בִּמְרוֹמָיו, הוּא יַעֲשֶׂה שָׁלוֹם עָלֵינוּ וְעַל כָּל יִשְׂרָאֵל וְאִמְרוּ, אָמֵן.

Oseh shalom bi-m'romav, hu ya'aseh shalom aleinu ve-al kol Yisrael,
ve-imru, Amen.

• Make up your own blessing, thanking God for this seder.

כּוֹס שְׁלִישִׁי
Kos Sh'lishi
The Third Cup

The meal may be over, but the seder isn't.

The leader recites the blessing over the third cup of wine or grape juice:

בָּרוּךְ אַתָּה יהוה אֱלֹהֵינוּ מֶלֶךְ הָעוֹלָם, בּוֹרֵא פְּרִי הַגָּפֶן.

Barukh atah Adonai eloheinu melekh ha-olam, borei p'ri ha-gafen.

Praised are You, Adonai our God, Ruler of the universe, Who creates the fruit of the vine.

Drink the wine or grape juice, leaning to the left. Refill the cup.

כּוֹס אֵלִיָּהוּ
Kos Eliyahu
The Cup of Elijah

The Cup of Elijah, a special goblet of wine reserved for the prophet Elijah, may either be filled now or before the seder begins. Legends tell us that Elijah visits every seder to provide for the poor and to announce an era of peace.

One such story is of two women, one poor and one rich. The poor woman washed her children's clothes by the river before Passover, but her heart was sad, for she had nothing for the festival. Suddenly an old man appeared. He asked her if she had everything prepared for the holiday. "Oh, yes," she answered, for she did not wish to complain. The next day, the rich woman washed her clothes by the riverbank. The same old man appeared and asked her the same question. "Nothing is prepared!" she grumbled bitterly, for she was never happy with what she had.

On the seder night, the poor woman did not have food on the table, nor even candles to light. But the table was set with a white cloth and the children were dressed in clean, bright clothes. Not so in the rich woman's house. There was much on the table, but her family complained and argued, and there was no happiness in their hearts.

Suddenly the old man appeared in the rich house and said, "On the bank of the river you told me you had prepared nothing for the holiday. That is what you'll have." The rich home became empty and dark.

The old man knocked on the door of the poor woman's house and said, "On the bank of the river you told me you had prepared everything for the holiday. That is what you'll have." In an instant the poor woman's home was filled with light and happiness, love and songs, and lots of good food.

When she looked over at the rich woman's house, where there was no light or festivity, the poor woman realized her neighbor didn't have a seder. She invited the rich woman and her family to be guests in her home. Together they celebrated Passover in friendship and hospitality.

The poor woman wanted to thank the old man who had brought these miracles, but he had disappeared. Then she knew that he was none other than Elijah the Prophet.

Open the door for Elijah and sing together:

אֵלִיָּהוּ הַנָּבִיא, אֵלִיָּהוּ הַתִּשְׁבִּי,
אֵלִיָּהוּ, אֵלִיָּהוּ, אֵלִיָּהוּ הַגִּלְעָדִי,
בִּמְהֵרָה בְיָמֵינוּ יָבֹא אֵלֵינוּ
עִם מָשִׁיחַ בֶּן דָּוִד.
עִם מָשִׁיחַ בֶּן דָּוִד.

Eliyahu ha-Navi,
Eliyahu ha-Tishbi.
Eliyahu, Eliyahu, Eliyahu ha-Giladi.
Bi-m'herah be-yameinu yavo eleinu,
im mashiaḥ ben David,
im mashiaḥ ben David.

We hope that Elijah the Prophet comes soon.
Watch to see if any wine disappears from the goblet!

הַלֵּל
Hallel
Sing Songs of Praise

The whole world praises God. God's love for us lasts forever.

הַלְלוּ אֶת יהוה כָּל גּוֹיִם, שַׁבְּחוּהוּ כָּל הָאֻמִּים.
כִּי גָבַר עָלֵינוּ חַסְדּוֹ, וֶאֱמֶת יהוה לְעוֹלָם הַלְלוּיָהּ.
הוֹדוּ לַיהוה כִּי טוֹב, כִּי לְעוֹלָם חַסְדּוֹ.
יֹאמַר נָא יִשְׂרָאֵל, כִּי לְעוֹלָם חַסְדּוֹ.
יֹאמְרוּ נָא בֵית אַהֲרֹן, כִּי לְעוֹלָם חַסְדּוֹ.
יֹאמְרוּ נָא יִרְאֵי יהוה, כִּי לְעוֹלָם חַסְדּוֹ.

Hallelu et Adonai kol goyim, shab'ḥuhu kol ha-umim.
Ki gavar aleinu ḥasdo, ve-emet Adonai le-olam, halleluyah.
Hodu l'Adonai ki tov, ki le-olam ḥasdo.
Yomar na Yisrael, ki le-olam ḥasdo.
Yomar na veit Aharon, ki le-olam ḥasdo.
Yomar na yir'ei Adonai, ki le-olam ḥasdo.

Hodu La-Shem

If you're sleepy, this song is sure to wake you up!

Divide into two groups:
Whenever the words *Hallelu* or *Halleluyah* (praise) come up, Group #1 stands and sings. Whenever the words *hodu la-Shem* (let's thank God) come up, Group #2 stands and sings. The group that isn't singing should sit down.

Repeat twice:
Group #1: *Hallelu* (three times) *Halleluyah*
Group #2: *Hodu la-Shem*

Repeat three times:
Group #2: *Hodu la-Shem*
Group #1: *Halleluyah*
Group #2: *Hodu la-Shem*

Hodu La-Shem

Traditional

Lyrics under the music:

Ha-le-lu Ha-le-lu Ha-le-lu Ha-le-lu-yah ho-du la-Shem. Ha-le-

lu Ha-le-lu Ha-le-lu Ha-le-lu-yah ho-du la-Shem.

Ho-du la-Shem Ha-le-lu-yah Ho-du la-Shem Ha-le-lu-yah

Ho-du la-Shem Ha-le-lu-yah Ho-du la-Shem Ha-le

• Go around the table and let everyone tell what they're thankful for.

כּוֹס רְבִיעִי
Kos Revi'i
The Fourth Cup

The leader raises the fourth cup of wine and says:

בָּרוּךְ אַתָּה יהוה אֱלֹהֵינוּ מֶלֶךְ הָעוֹלָם, בּוֹרֵא פְּרִי הַגָּפֶן.

Barukh atah Adonai eloheinu melekh ha-olam, borei p'ri ha-gafen.

Praised are You, Adonai our God, Ruler of the universe, Who creates the fruit of the vine.

Drink the wine, leaning to the left.

זְמִירוֹת
Z'mirot
Songs

אַדִּיר הוּא
Adir Hu
God Is Mighty

Adir Hu is an ABC song in Hebrew that tells of God's greatness and power. God is **a**wesome, **b**lessed, **c**aring, **d**ivine, **e**xcellent, **f**aithful, **g**lorious, and **h**oly. . . . Each word begins with the next letter of the Hebrew alphabet. The chorus asks God to bring a time of peace to the world.

אַדִּיר הוּא, יִבְנֶה בֵיתוֹ בְּקָרוֹב, בִּמְהֵרָה בִּמְהֵרָה,
בְּיָמֵינוּ בְּקָרוֹב. אֵל בְּנֵה, אֵל בְּנֵה, בְּנֵה בֵיתְךָ בְּקָרוֹב.

בָּחוּר הוּא, גָּדוֹל הוּא, דָּגוּל הוּא, יִבְנֶה בֵיתוֹ בְּקָרוֹב,
בִּמְהֵרָה בִּמְהֵרָה, בְּיָמֵינוּ בְּקָרוֹב, אֵל בְּנֵה, אֵל בְּנֵה,
בְּנֵה בֵיתְךָ בְּקָרוֹב.

הָדוּר הוּא, וָתִיק הוּא, זַכַּאי הוּא, יִבְנֶה בֵיתוֹ בְּקָרוֹב,
בִּמְהֵרָה בִּמְהֵרָה, בְּיָמֵינוּ בְּקָרוֹב, אֵל בְּנֵה, אֵל בְּנֵה,
בְּנֵה בֵיתְךָ בְּקָרוֹב.

חָסִיד הוּא, טָהוֹר הוּא, יָחִיד הוּא, יִבְנֶה בֵיתוֹ בְּקָרוֹב,
בִּמְהֵרָה בִּמְהֵרָה, בְּיָמֵינוּ בְּקָרוֹב, אֵל בְּנֵה, אֵל בְּנֵה,
בְּנֵה בֵיתְךָ בְּקָרוֹב.

כַּבִּיר הוּא, לָמוּד הוּא, מֶלֶךְ הוּא, יִבְנֶה בֵיתוֹ בְּקָרוֹב,
בִּמְהֵרָה בִּמְהֵרָה, בְּיָמֵינוּ בְּקָרוֹב, אֵל בְּנֵה, אֵל בְּנֵה,
בְּנֵה בֵיתְךָ בְּקָרוֹב.

Chorus:

Adir hu, yivneh veito be-karov, bi-m'herah, bi-m'herah
be-yameinu be-karov. El b'neh, el b'neh, b'neh veitkha be-karov.

1. *Baḥur hu, gadol hu, dagul hu, yivneh veito be-karov . . .*
2. *Hadur hu, vatik hu, zakkai hu . . .*
3. *Ḥassid hu, tahor hu, yaḥid hu . . .*
4. *Kabir hu, lamud hu, melekh hu . . .*
5. *Nora hu, saggiv hu, izzuz hu . . .*
6. *Podeh hu, tzaddik hu, kadosh hu . . .*
7. *Raḥum hu, shaddai hu, takif hu . . .*

אֶחָד מִי יוֹדֵעַ
Eḥad Mi Yode'a
Who Knows One?

This is a counting song. Each number, from one to thirteen, represents something wonderful the Jewish people have or do.

Who knows one? I know one.
One is our God, Who is in heaven and on earth.
Two are the tablets of the law.
Three are the fathers: Abraham, Isaac, and Jacob.
Four are the mothers: Sarah, Rebecca, Rachel, and Leah.
Five are the books of the Torah.
Six are the books of the *Mishnah* (Jewish law).
Seven are the days of the week.
Eight are the days of *brit milah* (circumcision).
Nine are the months of pregnancy.
Ten are the Ten Commandments.
Eleven are the stars in Joseph's dream.
Twelve are the tribes of Israel.
Thirteen are the qualities of God—kind, caring, truthful, forgiving, and more.

(As you sing each new line, count backward by adding the lines above, beginning with the numbers in red.)

אֶחָד מִי יוֹדֵעַ? אֶחָד אֲנִי יוֹדֵעַ: אֶחָד אֱלֹהֵינוּ שֶׁבַּשָּׁמַיִם וּבָאָרֶץ.

שְׁנַיִם מִי יוֹדֵעַ? שְׁנַיִם אֲנִי יוֹדֵעַ: שְׁנֵי לֻחוֹת הַבְּרִית...

שְׁלֹשָׁה מִי יוֹדֵעַ? שְׁלֹשָׁה אֲנִי יוֹדֵעַ: שְׁלֹשָׁה אָבוֹת...

אַרְבַּע מִי יוֹדֵעַ? אַרְבַּע אֲנִי יוֹדֵעַ: אַרְבַּע אִמָּהוֹת...

חֲמִשָּׁה מִי יוֹדֵעַ? חֲמִשָּׁה אֲנִי יוֹדֵעַ: חֲמִשָּׁה חֻמְשֵׁי תוֹרָה...

שִׁשָּׁה מִי יוֹדֵעַ? שִׁשָּׁה אֲנִי יוֹדֵעַ: שִׁשָּׁה סִדְרֵי מִשְׁנָה...

שִׁבְעָה מִי יוֹדֵעַ? שִׁבְעָה אֲנִי יוֹדֵעַ: שִׁבְעָה יְמֵי שַׁבַּתָּא...

שְׁמוֹנָה מִי יוֹדֵעַ? שְׁמוֹנָה אֲנִי יוֹדֵעַ: שְׁמוֹנָה יְמֵי מִילָה...

תִּשְׁעָה מִי יוֹדֵעַ? תִּשְׁעָה אֲנִי יוֹדֵעַ: תִּשְׁעָה יַרְחֵי לֵידָה...

עֲשָׂרָה מִי יוֹדֵעַ? עֲשָׂרָה אֲנִי יוֹדֵעַ: עֲשָׂרָה דִבְּרַיָּא...

אַחַד עָשָׂר מִי יוֹדֵעַ? אַחַד עָשָׂר אֲנִי יוֹדֵעַ: אַחַד עָשָׂר כּוֹכְבַיָּא...

שְׁנֵים עָשָׂר מִי יוֹדֵעַ? שְׁנֵים עָשָׂר אֲנִי יוֹדֵעַ: שְׁנֵים עָשָׂר שִׁבְטַיָּא...

שְׁלֹשָׁה עָשָׂר מִי יוֹדֵעַ? שְׁלֹשָׁה עָשָׂר אֲנִי יוֹדֵעַ: שְׁלֹשָׁה עָשָׂר מִדַּיָּא, שְׁנֵים עָשָׂר שִׁבְטַיָּא, אַחַד עָשָׂר כּוֹכְבַיָּא, עֲשָׂרָה דִבְּרַיָּא, תִּשְׁעָה יַרְחֵי לֵידָה, שְׁמוֹנָה יְמֵי מִילָה, שִׁבְעָה יְמֵי שַׁבַּתָּא, שִׁשָּׁה סִדְרֵי מִשְׁנָה, חֲמִשָּׁה חֻמְשֵׁי תוֹרָה, אַרְבַּע אִמָּהוֹת, שְׁלֹשָׁה אָבוֹת, שְׁנֵי לֻחוֹת הַבְּרִית, אֶחָד אֱלֹהֵינוּ שֶׁבַּשָּׁמַיִם וּבָאָרֶץ.

Eḥad mi yode'a? Eḥad ani yode'a.
Eḥad Eloheinu she-ba-shamayim u-va-aretz.
Sh'nayim mi yode'a? Sh'nayim ani yode'a.
Sh'nei luḥot ha-b'rit, eḥad Eloheinu she-ba-shamayim u-va-aretz.
Sh'loshah avot,
Arbah imahot,
Ḥamishah ḥumshei Torah,
Shishah sidrei mishnah,
Shiv'ah y'mei shabata,
Sh'monah y'mei milah,
Tishah yarḥei leidah,
Asarah dibraya,
Aḥad asar kokhvaya,
Sh'neim asar shivtaya,
Sh'loshah asar midaya.

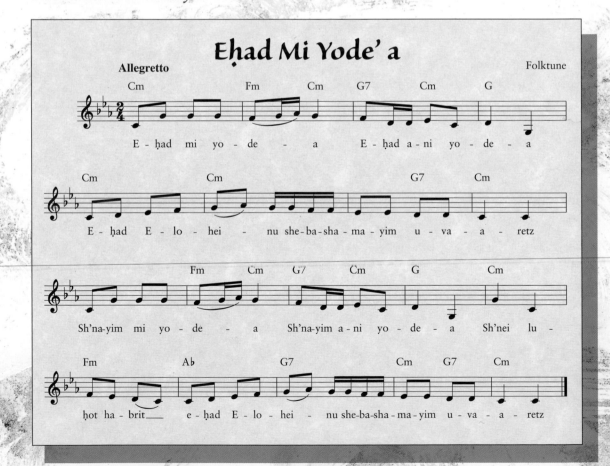

Eḥad Mi Yode' a

Allegretto

Folktune

Jews in Spain, Portugal, Turkey, Greece, and Yugoslavia sing this version of *Eḥad Mi Yode'a* to a different tune in a different language—Ladino—a mixture of Spanish and Hebrew. Try it for fun!

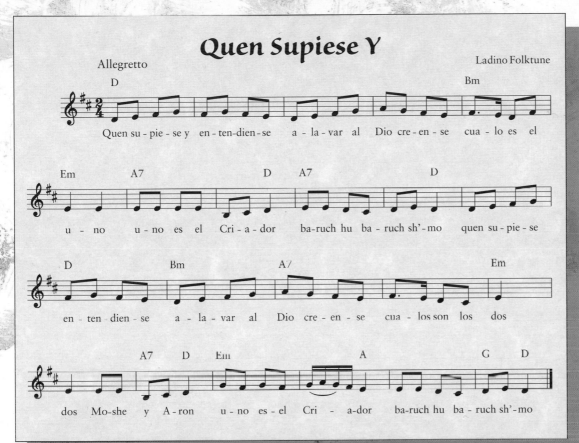

Quen Supiese Y

Allegretto

Ladino Folktune

Quen supiese y entendiense, alavar al Dio cre'ense cualo es el uno?
Uno es el Cri'ador, Barukh hu barukh shemo.

Quen supiese y entendiense, alavar al Dio cre'ense cualo son los dos?
Dos Moshe y Aron, uno es el Cri'ador . . .

Cualo son los tres? Tres padres muestros son, Avram, Itzhak, y Ya'kov,
dos Moshe y Aron . . .

Cualo son los quatro? Quatro madres muestras son, Sarah, Rivkah,
Raḥel, Leah, tres padres muestros son . . .

• Create your own counting song! Here is an example:

One is our family . . . Two are our parents . . . Three are our pets. . . .

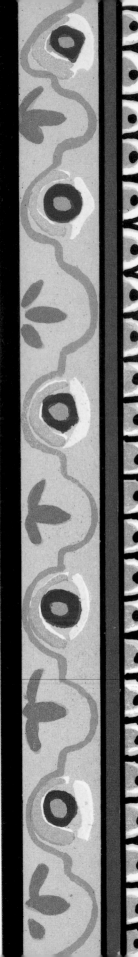

חַד גַּדְיָא
Ḥad Gadya
Just One Kid

No, this is not a song about an only child. It's a song about a baby goat that a father bought for two coins, two *zuzim*. It may sound like a nursery rhyme, but it has a much deeper meaning. The father is God, who buys the "kid," Israel, with two tablets, the Ten Commandments. But then, all kinds of enemies chase each other. Let's see who wins!

• Try to make the sounds of each character, or act out the song.

First, a cat (*meow*) came and ate the kid (*baa*),
then a dog (*woof, woof*) came and bit the cat,
a stick beat the dog,
a fire burnt the stick,
water put out the fire,
an ox drank the water,
a butcher killed the ox,
the angel of death killed the butcher,
and finally, God killed the angel of death.

Even though Israel has had—and still has—a lot of enemies,
God saves us in the end.

חַד גַּדְיָא, חַד גַּדְיָא.

(Repeat this line in red at the end of each verse) דְּזַבִּין אַבָּא בִּתְרֵי זוּזֵי, חַד גַּדְיָא חַד גַּדְיָא.

וְאָתָא שׁוּנְרָא וְאָכְלָה לְגַדְיָא...

וְאָתָא כַלְבָּא וְנָשַׁךְ לְשׁוּנְרָא, דְּאָכְלָה לְגַדְיָא,...

וְאָתָא חוּטְרָא וְהִכָּה לְכַלְבָּא, דְּנָשַׁךְ לְשׁוּנְרָא דְּאָכְלָה לְגַדְיָא,...

וְאָתָא נוּרָא וְשָׂרַף לְחוּטְרָא, דְּהִכָּה לְכַלְבָּא, דְּנָשַׁךְ לְשׁוּנְרָא, דְּאָכְלָה לְגַדְיָא,...

וְאָתָא מַיָּא וְכָבָה לְנוּרָא, דְּשָׂרַף לְחוּטְרָא, דְּהִכָּה לְכַלְבָּא, דְּנָשַׁךְ לְשׁוּנְרָא דְּאָכְלָה לְגַדְיָא,...

וְאָתָא תוֹרָא וְשָׁתָה לְמַיָּא, דְּכָבָה לְנוּרָא, דְּשָׂרַף לְחוּטְרָא, דְּהִכָּה לְכַלְבָּא, דְּנָשַׁךְ לְשׁוּנְרָא, דְּאָכְלָה לְגַדְיָא,...

וְאָתָא הַשּׁוֹחֵט וְשָׁחַט לְתוֹרָא, דְּשָׁתָה לְמַיָּא, דְּכָבָה לְנוּרָא, דְּשָׂרַף לְחוּטְרָא, דְּהִכָּה לְכַלְבָּא, דְּנָשַׁךְ לְשׁוּנְרָא, דְּאָכְלָה לְגַדְיָא,...

וְאָתָא מַלְאַךְ הַמָּוֶת וְשָׁחַט לְשׁוֹחֵט, דְּשָׁחַט לְתוֹרָא, דְּשָׁתָה לְמַיָּא, דְּכָבָה לְנוּרָא, דְּשָׂרַף לְחוּטְרָא, דְּהִכָּה לְכַלְבָּא, דְּנָשַׁךְ לְשׁוּנְרָא, דְּאָכְלָה לְגַדְיָא,...

וְאָתָא הַקָּדוֹשׁ בָּרוּךְ הוּא וְשָׁחַט לְמַלְאַךְ הַמָּוֶת, דְּשָׁחַט לְשׁוֹחֵט, דְּשָׁחַט לְתוֹרָא, דְּשָׁתָה לְמַיָּא, דְּכָבָה לְנוּרָא, דְּשָׂרַף לְחוּטְרָא, דְּהִכָּה לְכַלְבָּא, דְּנָשַׁךְ לְשׁוּנְרָא, דְּאָכְלָה לְגַדְיָא דְּזַבִּין אַבָּא בִּתְרֵי זוּזֵי, חַד גַּדְיָא חַד גַּדְיָא.

1. *Ḥad gadya, ḥad gadya*
De-zabin abba bi-trei zuzei, ḥad gadya, ḥad gadya.

Keep adding on a line, repeating the lines before it:
2. *Ve-ata shunra ve-akhla le-gadya,*
de-zabin abba bi-trei zuzei, ḥad gadya, ḥad gadya.

3. *Ve-ata khalba ve-nashakh le-shunra, de-akhla le-gadya, de-zabin . . .*
4. *Ve-ata ḥutra ve-hikah le-khalba, de-nashakh le-shunra, de-akhla le-gadya . . .*
5. *Ve-ata nura ve-saraf le-ḥutra, de-hikah le-khalba . . .*
6. *Ve-ata maya ve-khavah le-nura, de-saraf le-ḥutra . . .*
7. *Ve-ata tora ve-shatah le-maya, de-khavah le-nura . . .*
8. *Ve-ata ha-shoḥet ve-shaḥat le-tora, de-shatah le-maya . . .*
9. *Ve-ata malakh ha-mavet ve-shaḥat le-shoḥet, de-shaḥat le-tora . . .*
10. *Ve-ata Ha-Kadosh Barukh Hu ve-shaḥat le-malakh ha-mavet, de-shaḥat le-shoḥet . . .*

נִרְצָה
Nirtzah
End the Seder

Every good story comes to an end. We enjoyed every word, every sound, every picture it drew in our minds. We look forward to hearing it again. Between now and then, we hope for peace in the land of Israel and for freedom the world over.

I remember when we yearned for Jerusalem.
We prayed to touch its white-gold stones
when all we could feel was the cold dark cell of slavery.
We dreamed of breathing Jerusalem's pure air
when all we could smell was the stench of prison.
You whispered to me, "Don't give up hope!
Next year in Jerusalem!"
Now, as I watch kites soar across Jerusalem's golden sky,
I turn cartwheels across its white-gold streets
paved with voices singing together from all over the world,
Next year in Jerusalem!

לַשָׁנָה הַבָּאָה בִּירוּשָׁלָיִם

La-shanah ha-ba'ah b'Yerusalayim.

Next Year in Jerusalem!

With love to my family for the many joyous sedarim we have shared. To my parents, Rabbi Ezekiel and Margaret Musleah. To my sisters, Flora and Aliza, and my children, Shira and Shoshana. Special thanks to Rabbi Michael Klayman for his invaluable help.
—R. M.

To Alon, Caitlin, Tal, and Jolie—with love from Grandma
—L. A.

Art note:
The artwork is a combination of lino cuts printed in oil on rice paper with added multimedia treatments.

All Kalaniot Books have accompanying activity guides. Download them for free at KalaniotBooks.com.

Text copyright © 2000 by Rahel Musleah
Illustrations copyright © 2000 by Louise August

Originally published in 2000 by Simon & Schuster Children's Publishing

This edition published in 2024 by Kalaniot Books,
an imprint of Endless Mountains Publishing Company
72 Glenmaura National Boulevard, Suite 104B, Moosic, Pennsylvania 18507
www.KalaniotBooks.com

Library of Congress Control Number: 2023943327
ISBN: 979-8-9863965-5-2
Printed in China
First Printing

Reprinted with permission from Tara Publications:
"Kadesh Urḥatz"
"Mah Nishtanah"
"Avadim Hayinu"
"Dayyenu"
"Ve-nomar Lefanav"
"Eliyahu Hanavi"
"Hodu La-Shem"
"Adir Hu"
"Eḥad Mi Yode'a"
"Quen Supiese Y"
"Ḥad Gadya"

Reprinted with permission of Random House, Inc., from *Holocaust Poetry*: "Ani Maamin: A Song Lost and Found Again" by Elie Wiesel © 1973

Reprinted with permission from Sounds Write Productions, Inc. (ASCAP): "Miriam's Song" by Debbie Friedman © 1988 Lyrics based on Exodus 15:20-21

Reprinted with permission from Leah Abrams, from *Apples on Holidays and Other Days*: "Out of Egypt" by Leah Abrams © 1988

Reprinted with permission of the publisher, Jason Aronson Inc., Northvale, NJ © 1991: Adaptation of "The Neighbors" from *Tales of Elijah the Prophet* by Peninnah Schram

Reprinted with permission from Claudia Roden: Recipe for "Tishpishti: Turkish Nut Cake"

The Hebrew text has been checked against *The Feast of Freedom*, the haggadah published by The Rabbinical Assembly (1982). In a few instances, I have chosen to use another text version. The short version of the *Birkat Hamazon*, the Blessings after the Meal, is widely used by the Conservative movement, and is based on a version that appears in one of the oldest existing prayer books, the siddur of Saadia Gaon, dating from the tenth century.
R. M.